D0090323

THE
WISDOM
OF THE
NATIVE
AMERICANS

THE

WISDOM

OF THE

NATIVE

AMERICANS

COMPILED AND EDITED BY
KENT NERBURN

NEW WORLD LIBRARY
NOVATO, CALIFORNIA

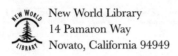 New World Library
14 Pamaron Way
Novato, California 94949

Library of Congress Cataloging-in-Publication Data
Wisdom of the native Americans: includes the soul of an Indian
    and other writings by Ohiyesa, and the great speeches of Red
    Jacket, Chief Joseph, and Chief Seattle / edited by Kent
    Nerburn.
        p.   cm.
    ISBN 1-57731-079-9 (alk. paper)
    1. Indian philosophy — North American. 2. Speeches, addresses,
etc., Indian — North America. 3. Indians of North America —
Quotations. I. Nerburn, Kent, 1946– .
E98.P5W57   1999
970.004'97—dc21   98-42936
                                                       CIP

First printing, March 1999
ISBN 1-57731-079-9
Printed in the U.S.A. on acid-free, recycled paper
Distributed to the trade by Publishers Group West

10 9 8 7 6 5 4 3

"Let us put our minds together and see what kind of life we can make for our children."

— Sitting Bull

TABLE OF CONTENTS

INTRODUCTION

In 1492 Columbus and his crew, lost, battered, and stricken with dysentery, were helped ashore by a people he described as "neither black nor white . . . fairly tall, good looking and well proportioned." Believing he had landed in the East Indies, he called these people Indians. In fact, they were part of a great population that had made its home on this continent for centuries.

The inhabitants of this land were not one people. Their customs differed. Their languages differed. Some tilled the earth; others hunted and picked the abundance of the land around them. They lived in

different kinds of housing and governed themselves according to differing rules.

But they shared in common a belief that the earth is a spiritual presence that must be honored, not mastered. Unfortunately, western Europeans who came to these shores had a contrary belief. To them, the entire American continent was a beautiful but savage land that it was not only their right but their duty to tame and use as they saw fit.

As we enter the twenty-first century, Western civilization is confronting the inevitable results of this European-American philosophy of dominance. We have gotten out of balance with our earth, and the very future of our planet depends on our capacity to restore the balance.

We are crying out for help, for a grounding in the truth of nature, for words of wisdom. That wisdom is here, contained in the words of the native peoples of the Americas. But these people speak quietly. Their words are simple and their voices soft. We have not heard them because we have not taken the time to listen. Perhaps now the time is right for us to open our ears and hearts to the words they have to say.

Unlike many traditions, the spiritual wisdom of the Native Americans is not found in a set of "scriptural" materials. It is, and always has been, a part of the fabric of daily life and experience. One of the most poignant reflections of this spiritual message is found in their tradition of oratory.

Traditionally, Indians did not carry on dialogues when discussing important matters. Rather, each person listened attentively until his or her turn came to speak, and then he or she rose and spoke without interruption about the heart of the matter under consideration. This tradition produced a measured eloquence of speech and thought that is almost unmatched for its clarity and simplicity.

Indian reasoning about governmental and social affairs was also carried on with the same uncompromising purity of insight and expression.

It is from these orations, recorded observations of life and social affairs, and other first-person testimonies that the materials for this book have been drawn. The wisdom has been available for some time, but much of it has been recorded only in imposing governmental documents and arcane academic treatises.

The Wisdom of the Native Americans gathers three of New World Library's volumes of Indian oration into one collection. In addition to the short, distilled passages of *Native American Wisdom,* a smaller volume I compiled with Louise Mengelkoch, this book includes the thoughts of one of the most fascinating and overlooked individuals in American history: Ohiyesa, also known by the Anglicized name of Charles Alexander Eastman.

Ohiyesa was, at heart, a poet of the spirit and the bearer of spiritual wisdom. To the extent that he dared, and with increasing fervor as he aged, he was a preacher for the native vision of life. It is my considered belief it is his spiritual vision, above all else, that we of our generation need to hear. We hunger for the words and insights of the Native American, and no man spoke with more clarity than Ohiyesa.

Ohiyesa was born in southern Minnesota in the area now called Redwood Falls in the winter of 1858. He was a member of the Dakota, or Sioux, nation. When he was four, his people rose up in desperation against the U.S. Government, which was systematically starving them by withholding provisions and payment they were owed from the sale of their land.

When their uprising was crushed, more that a thousand men, women, and children were captured and taken away. On the day after Christmas in 1862, thirty-eight of the men were hanged at Mankato, Minnesota, in the greatest mass execution ever performed by the U.S. Government. Those who were not killed were taken to stockades and holding camps, where they faced starvation and death during the icy days of the northern winter.

Ohiyesa's father, Many Lightnings, was among those captured.

Ohiyesa, who was among those left behind, was handed over to his uncle to be raised in the traditional Sioux manner. He was taught the ways of the forest and lessons of his people. He strove to become a hunter and a warrior. Then, one day while he was hunting, he saw an Indian walking toward him in white man's clothes. It was his father, who had survived the internment camps and had returned to claim his son.

During his incarceration, Many Lightnings had seen the power of the European culture and had become convinced that the Indian way of life could not survive within it. He despised what he called "reservation Indians" who gave up their independence and tradition in order to accept a handout from the European conquerors.

He took Ohiyesa to a small plot of farming land in eastern South Dakota and began teaching him to be a new type of warrior. He sent him off to white schools with the admonition that "it is the same as if I sent you on your first warpath. I shall expect you to conquer."

Thus was born Charles Alexander Eastman, the Santee Sioux child of the woodlands and prairies who would go on to become the adviser to presidents and an honored member of New England society.

Ohiyesa, or Eastman, went to Beloit College where he learned English and immersed himself in the culture and ways of the white world. Upon graduation he went east. He attended Dartmouth College, then was accepted into medical school at Boston University, which he completed in 1890. He returned to his native Midwest to work among his own people as a physician on the Pine Ridge reservation, but became disenchanted with the corruption of the U.S. government and its Indian agents. After a short-lived effort to establish a private medical practice in St. Paul, Minnesota, he turned his focus back to the issue of Indian-white relations.

For the next twenty-five years, he was involved in various efforts to build bridges of understanding between the Indians and non-Indian people of America. He worked first for the YMCA, then served as an attorney for his people in Washington, then returned to South Dakota to spend three years as physician for the Sioux at Crow Creek.

In 1903 he went back to Massachusetts and devoted himself to bringing the voice of the Indian into the American intellectual arena. He became deeply involved in the Boy Scout program, believing it was the best way to give non-Indian American youth a sense of the wonder and values that he had learned growing up in the wild.

Eventually, with the help of his wife, he established a camp of his own in New Hampshire in which he tried to recreate the experience of Sioux education and values for non-Indian children.

But financial troubles and the fundamentally irreconcilable differences between Indian culture and white civilization ultimately took their toll. In 1918 he and his white wife separated, and in 1921 he left New England for good. He continued to believe that the way of civilization was the way of the future, but he had lost much of his faith in its capacity to speak to the higher moral and spiritual vision of humanity. He returned again to his native forests of the Midwest, devoting more time to his traditional ways, often going into the woods alone for months at a time.

But he never ceased believing that the two cultures that had clashed so tragically on the soil of the American continent somehow had to become one if there ever was to be a true America with an honest and indigenous soul. Even though he had come to believe that white civilization was, at heart, "a system of life based on trade," he still felt that it was the task of the best people, both Indian and non-Indian, to help America find a shared vision. As he said at the end of his autobiography, *From Deep Woods to Civilization*, "I am an Indian; and while I have learned much from civilization, for which I am grateful, I have never lost my Indian sense of right and justice. I am for development and progress along social and spiritual lines, rather than those of commerce, nationalism, or efficiency. Nevertheless, so long as I live, I am an American."

As an observer of Indian life, Ohiyesa was unlike

any other. He was at once completely secure in his Indian identity, yet gave himself over completely to the search for meaning within the context of a European America. He tried with his whole heart and spirit to believe in the wisdom of each of the ways he had learned. If there was struggle, it was because the two ways coexisted so uneasily within one person.

Though he lamented the passing of the Indian ways, he accepted it as the workings of the Great Mystery, and set himself to the dual task of bringing the ways of the whites to the Indians and the ways of the Indians to the whites. He never lost his grounding in his traditional ways, even while exploring the intricacies of "the Christ Ideal" and dining with presidents. He was ever the observer, journeying ever deeper into the ways of white culture, trying, as his grandmother had always instructed him, "to follow a new trail to the point of knowing."

The writings he has left are the documents of that journey, crafted by a man with a warrior's heart, an orator's tongue, and human spirit of such dignity that it transcends boundaries of race and belief.

Like much of the material here, the third part of this volume — the great speeches of Chiefs Red Jacket, Joseph, and Seattle — is best approached with an understanding of the Indian oral tradition these speeches represent.

Most of us are trained to read with our minds. We pass over words, compressing them into ideas, and we use these ideas as the measure of our understanding. But there is another way to read, where the words themselves take on a life of their own, and the rhythms and cadences open a floodgate of images and sympathies, until we feel the heartbeat of their author and sense the lifeblood of experience that they contain.

It is a way of reading that is more akin to listening to music, where the sheer power of the sound can move the hearer to tears.

This is the way we should read these great speeches. Like the insistent beat of ceremonial drums, their words weave a hypnotic spell, and the passion of their vision enters into the hearts as well as the minds of their listeners.

These speeches are the songs of the spirit of great men who spoke for a great people. In their words, between their words, beneath and above their words, is the love, the faith, the anger, and the pathos of a people who believed in the ways of their ancestors and could not make these ways understood to the European settlers who were so intent upon changing them.

Today the battle is over. This continent is, at least on the surface, a distant mirror of the European continent, controlled in its shape and direction by the descendants of the Europeans who were once raw immigrants on its shores.

But the spirit of the Native people, the first people, has never died. It lives in the rocks and the forests, the rivers and the mountains. It murmurs in the brooks and whispers in the trees.

The hearts of these people were formed of the earth that we now walk, and their voice can never be silenced. The three speeches gathered here give us a chance to hear that voice again.

The selection of these particular speeches was made with care and love. I could have chosen more; I could have chosen otherwise. But these three, each imbued with its own individual genius, work together in a way that is almost transcendent in its poignancy and beauty.

Red Jacket's speech shows us the strength and faith of the traditional way, and stands like an oak against the coming storms of the European. Chief Joseph's speech takes us along on the journey of a people from free, loving, and hopeful children of the land to a fugitive remnant pursued through forests and mountains into a tragic submission on the windswept foothills of the Rockies. Chief Seattle's speech begins as an eloquent eulogy to the Indian people, but soon rises to become an admonition to us all, and a bonding together of the Indian and non-Indian into a common fate.

In the course of the three, we are carried along from the sunrise hopes of the Native peoples as they offered the hand of friendship to a new and foreign visitor, to the sunset of their dreams as this visitor grew in number and in strength and betrayed the friendship with which he had been met, to the dawning of a new era in which we all must learn the lessons of the Native people if we are to live honorably upon this land we all now share.

These are wise men. They have much to teach. If we listen carefully, with good heart, they may teach us. I hope so, for we, as a nation, still have much to learn.

— *Kent Nerburn*
Bemidji, Minnesota

"There is a dignity about the social intercourse of old Indians which reminds me of a stroll through a winter forest."

— Frederick Remington

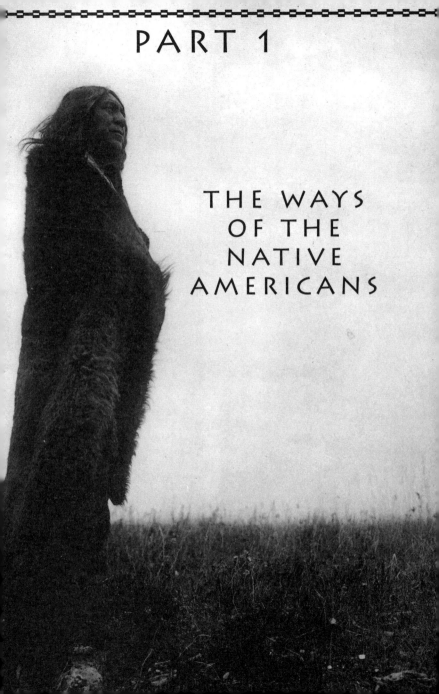

PART 1

THE WAYS OF THE NATIVE AMERICANS

THE WAYS OF THE LAND

"All things are connected. Whatever befalls the earth befalls the children of the earth."

— *Chief Seattle*
Suqwamish and Duwamish

I was born in Nature's wide domain! The trees were all that sheltered my infant limbs, the blue heavens all that covered me. I am one of Nature's children. I have always admired her. She shall be my glory: her features, her robes, and the wreath about her brow, the seasons, her stately oaks, and the evergreen — her hair, ringlets over the earth — all contribute to my enduring love of her.

And wherever I see her, emotions of pleasure roll in my breast, and swell and burst like waves on the shores of the ocean, in prayer and praise to Him who has placed me in her hand. It is thought great to be born in palaces, surrounded with wealth — but to be born in

Nature's wide domain is greater still!

I would much more glory in this birthplace, with the broad canopy of heaven above me, and the giant arms of the forest trees for my shelter, than to be born in palaces of marble, studded with pillars of gold! Nature will be Nature still, while palaces shall decay and fall in ruins.

Yes, Niagara will be Niagara a thousand years hence! The rainbow, a wreath over her brow, shall continue as long as the sun, and the flowing of the river — while the work of art, however carefully protected and preserved, shall fade and crumble into dust!

— George Copway (Kahgegagahbowh)
Ojibwe

What is man without the beasts? If all the beasts were gone, men would die from great loneliness of spirit, for whatever happens to the beasts also happens to man. All things are connected. Whatever befalls the earth befalls the children of the earth.

— Chief Seattle
Suqwamish and Duwamish

I love that land of winding waters more than all the rest of the world. A man who would not love his father's grave is worse than a wild animal.

— Chief Joseph
Nez Perce

The character of the Indian's emotion left little room in his heart for antagonism toward his fellow creatures. . . . For the Lakota [one of the three branches of the Sioux nation], mountains, lakes, rivers, springs, valleys, and woods were all finished beauty. Winds, rain, snow, sunshine, day, night, and change of seasons were endlessly fascinating. Birds, insects, and animals filled the world with knowledge that defied the comprehension of man.

The Lakota was a true naturalist — a lover of Nature. He loved the earth and all things of the earth, and the attachment grew with age. The old people came literally to love the soil and they sat or reclined on the ground with a feeling of being close to a mothering power.

It was good for the skin to touch the earth, and the old people liked to remove their moccasins and walk with bare feet on the sacred earth.

Their tipis were built upon the earth and their altars were made of earth. The birds that flew in the air came to rest upon the earth, and it was the final abiding place of all things that lived and grew. The soil was soothing, strengthening, cleansing, and healing.

This is why the old Indian still sits upon the earth instead of propping himself up and away from its life-giving forces. For him, to sit or lie upon the ground is to be able to think more deeply and to feel more keenly; he can see more clearly into the mysteries of life and come closer in kinship to other lives about him.

— *Chief Luther Standing Bear*
Teton Sioux

You ask me to plow the ground. Shall I take a knife and tear my mother's bosom? Then when I die she will not take me to her bosom to rest.

You ask me to dig for stones! Shall I dig under her skin for her bones? Then when I die I cannot enter her body to be born again.

You ask me to cut grass and make hay and sell it, and be rich like white men, but how dare I cut my mother's hair?

I want my people to stay with me here. All the dead men will come to life again. Their spirits will come to their bodies again. We must wait here in the homes of our fathers and be ready to meet them in the bosom of our mother.

— *Wovoka*
Paiute

Great Spirit — I want no blood upon my land to stain the grass. I want it all clear and pure, and I wish it so, that all who go through among my people may find it peaceful when they come, and leave peacefully when they go.

— *Ten Bears*
Yamparika Comanche

I love the land and the buffalo and will not part with it. . . .

I want the children raised as I was . . . I don't want to settle. I love to roam over the prairies. There I feel free and happy, but when we settle down we grow pale and die.

— *Satanta*
Kiowa Chief

2

THE WAYS OF WORDS AND SILENCE

"It does not require many words to speak the truth."

— *Chief Joseph*
Nez Perce

Silence was meaningful with the Lakota, and his granting a space of silence before talking was done in the practice of true politeness and regardful of the rule that "thought comes before speech."

And in the midst of sorrow, sickness, death, or misfortune of any kind, and in the presence of the notable and great, silence was the mark of respect. More powerful than words was silence with the Lakota.

His strict observance of this tenet of good behavior was the reason, no doubt, for his being given the false characterization by the white man of being a stoic. He has been judged to be dumb, stupid,

indifferent, and unfeeling.

As a matter of truth, he was the most sympathetic of men, but his emotions of depth and sincerity were tempered with control. Silence meant to the Lakota what it meant to Disraeli when he said, "Silence is the mother of truth," for the silent man was ever to be trusted, while the man ever ready with speech was never taken seriously.

— *Chief Luther Standing Bear*
Teton Sioux

In my opinion, it was chiefly owing to their deep contemplation in their silent retreats in the days of youth that the old Indian orators acquired the habit of carefully arranging their thoughts.

They listened to the warbling of birds and noted the grandeur and the beauties of the forest. The majestic clouds — which appear like mountains of granite floating in the air — the golden tints of a summer evening sky, and all the changes of nature, possessed a mysterious significance.

All this combined to furnish ample matter for reflection to the contemplating youth.

— *Francis Assikinack (Blackbird)*
Ottawa

Because we are old, it may be thought that the memory of things may be lost with us, who have not, like you, the art of preserving it by committing all transactions to writing.

We nevertheless have methods of transmitting from father to son an account of all these things. You will find the remembrance of them is faithfully preserved, and our succeeding generations are made acquainted with what has passed, that it may not be forgot as long as the earth remains.

— *Kanickhungo*
Treaty negotiations with Six Nations

You must speak straight so that your words may go as sunlight into our hearts.

— *Cochise ("Like Ironweed")*
Chiricahua Chief

A treaty, in the minds of our people, is an eternal word. Events often make it seem expedient to depart from the pledged word, but we are conscious that the first departure creates a logic for the second departure, until there is nothing left of the word.

— Declaration of Indian Purpose (1961)
American Indian Chicago Conference

How smooth must be the language of the whites, when they can make right look like wrong, and wrong like right.

— *Black Hawk*
Sauk

My father, you have made promises to me and to my children. If the promises had been made by a person of no standing, I should not be surprised to see his promises fail. But you, who are so great in riches and in power, I am astonished that I do not see your promises fulfilled!

I would have been better pleased if you had never made such promises, than that you should have made them and not performed them. . . .

— *Shinguaconse ("Little Pine")*

3

THE WAYS OF LEARNING

"Knowledge was inherent in all things. The world was a library. . . ."

— *Chief Luther Standing Bear*
Oglala Sioux

L ook at me — I am poor and naked, but I am the chief of the nation. We do not want riches, but we do want to train our children right. Riches would do us no good. We could not take them with us to the other world. We do not want riches. We want peace and love.

— *Red Cloud*
Sioux

You who are so wise must know that different nations have different conceptions of things. You will not therefore take it amiss if our ideas of the white man's kind of education happens not to be the same as yours.

We have had some experience of it.

Several of our young people were brought up in your colleges. They were instructed in all your sciences; but, when they came back to us, they were bad runners, ignorant of every means of living in the woods, unable to bear either cold or hunger. They didn't know how to build a cabin, take a deer, or kill an enemy. They spoke our language imperfectly.

They were therefore unfit to be hunters, warriors, or counselors; they were good for nothing.

We are, however, not the less obliged for your kind offer, though we decline accepting it. To show our gratefulness, if the gentlemen of Virginia shall send us a dozen of their sons, we will take great care with their education, instruct them in all we know, and make men of them.

> — *Canassatego*
> Treaty of Lancaster

Children were taught that true politeness was to be defined in actions rather than in words. They were never allowed to pass between the fire and an older person or a visitor, to speak while others were speaking, or to make fun of a crippled or disfigured person. If a child thoughtlessly tried to do so, a parent, in a quiet voice, immediately set him right.

Expressions such as "excuse me," "pardon me,"

and "so sorry," now so often lightly and unnecessarily used, are not in the Lakota language. If one chanced to injure or cause inconvenience to another, the word *wanunhecun,* or "mistake," was spoken. This was sufficient to indicate that no discourtesy was intended and that what had happened was accidental.

Our young people, raised under the old rules of courtesy, never indulged in the present habit of talking incessantly and all at the same time. To do so would have been not only impolite, but foolish; for poise, so much admired as a social grace, could not be accompanied by restlessness. Pauses were acknowledged gracefully and did not cause lack of ease or embarrassment.

In talking to children, the old Lakota would place a hand on the ground and explain: "We sit in the lap of our Mother. From her we, and all other living things, come. We shall soon pass, but the place where we now rest will last forever." So we, too, learned to sit or lie on the ground and become conscious of life about us in its multitude of forms.

Sometimes we boys would sit motionless and watch the swallows, the tiny ants, or perhaps some small animal at its work and ponder its industry and ingenuity; or we lay on our backs and looked long at the sky, and when the stars came out made shapes from the various groups.

Everything was possessed of personality, only differing from us in form. Knowledge was inherent in all things. The world was a library and its books were the stones, leaves, grass, brooks, and the birds and animals that shared, alike with us, the storms and blessings of earth. We learned to do what only the student of nature ever learns, and that was to feel beauty. We never railed at the storms, the furious winds, and the biting frosts and snows. To do so intensified human futility, so whatever came we adjusted ourselves, by more effort and energy if necessary, but without complaint.

Even the lightning did us no harm, for whenever it came too close, mothers and grandmothers in every tipi put cedar leaves on the coals and their magic kept danger away. Bright days and dark days were both expressions of the Great Mystery, and the Indian reveled in being close to the Great Holiness.

Observation was certain to have its rewards. Interest, wonder, admiration grew, and the fact was appreciated that life was more than mere human manifestation; it was expressed in a multitude of forms.

This appreciation enriched Lakota existence. Life was vivid and pulsing; nothing was casual and commonplace. The Indian lived — lived in every sense of the word — from his first to his last breath.

— *Chief Luther Standing Bear*
Teton Sioux

What boy would not be an Indian for a while when he thinks of the freest life in the world? We were close students of nature. We studied the habits of animals just as you study your books. We watched the men of our people and acted like them in our play, then learned to emulate them in our lives.

No people have better use of their five senses than the children of the wilderness. We could smell as well as hear and see. We could feel and taste as well as we could see and hear. Nowhere has the memory been more fully developed than in the wild life.

As a little child, it was instilled into me to be silent and reticent. This was one of the most important traits to form in the character of the Indian. As a hunter and warrior, it was considered absolutely necessary to him, and was thought to lay the foundations of patience and self-control. There are times when boisterous mirth is indulged in by our people, but the rule is gravity and decorum.

I wished to be a brave man as much as a white boy desires to be a great lawyer or even president of the United States.

I was made to respect the adults, especially the aged. I was not allowed to join in their discussions, or even to speak in their presence, unless requested to do so. Indian etiquette was very strict, and among the requirements was that of avoiding direct address. A term of relationship or some title of courtesy was commonly used instead of the personal name by those who wished to show respect.

We were taught generosity to the poor and reverence for the Great Mystery. Religion was the basis of all Indian training.

— *Charles Alexander Eastman (Ohiyesa)*
Santee Sioux

We send our little Indian boys and girls to school, and when they come back talking English, they come back swearing. There is no swear word in the Indian languages, and I haven't yet learned to swear.

— *Gertrude S. Bonnin (Zitkala-Sa)*
Yankton Sioux

4

THE WAYS OF LIVING

*"Our fathers gave us many laws, which they
had learned from their fathers. These laws were
good."*

— *Chief Joseph*
Nez Perce

P raise, flattery, exaggerated manners, and fine,
high-sounding words were no part of Lakota
politeness. Excessive manners were put down as insin-
cere, and the constant talker was considered rude and
thoughtless. Conversation was never begun at once, or
in a hurried manner.

No one was quick with a question, no matter how
important, and no one was pressed for an answer. A
pause giving time for thought was the truly courteous
way of beginning and conducting a conversation.

— *Chief Luther Standing Bear*
Teton Sioux

This is a happy season of the year — having plenty of provisions, such as beans, squashes, and other produce, with our dried meat and fish. We continue to make feasts and visit each other, until our corn is ripe.

At least one of the lodges in the village makes a feast daily for the Great Spirit. I cannot explain this so that the white people will comprehend me, because we have no regular standard among us. Everyone makes his feast as he thinks best, to please the Great Spirit, who has the care of all beings created.

— *Black Hawk*
Sauk

When you begin a great work you can't expect to finish it all at once; therefore do you and your brothers press on, and let nothing discourage you till you have entirely finished what you have begun.

Now, Brother, as for me, I assure you I will press on, and the contrary winds may blow strong in my face, yet I will go forward and never turn back, and continue to press forward until I have finished, and I would have you do the same. . . .

Though you may hear birds singing on this side and that side, you must not take notice of that, but hear me when I speak to you, and take it to heart, for you may always depend that what I say shall be true.

— *Teedyuscung*
Delaware

My young men shall never farm. Men who work the soil cannot dream, and wisdom comes to us in dreams.

— *Wowoka*
Paiute

If you ever get married, my son, do not make an idol of your wife. The more you worship her, the more she will want to be worshipped. . . . My son, this also I will tell you: Women should never be watched too closely. If you try to watch them, you will merely show your jealousy and become so jealous of your wife that she will leave you and run away. You yourself will be to blame for this.

— *Anonymous*
Winnebago

During the first year a newly married couple discovers whether they can agree with each other and can be happy — if not, they part, and look for other partners. If we were to live together and disagree, we should be as foolish as the whites.

No indiscretion can banish a woman from her parental lodge. It makes no difference how many children she may bring home; she is always welcome. The kettle is over the fire to feed them.

— *Black Hawk*
Sauk

Grandfather says that when your friends die you must not cry. You must not hurt anybody or do harm to anyone. You must not fight. Do right always. It will give you satisfaction in life.

— *Wovoka*
Paiute

We are all poor because we are all honest.

— *Red Dog*
Oglala Sioux

5

THE WAYS OF LEADING OTHERS

"No person among us desires any other reward for performing a brave and worthy action, but the consciousness of having served his nation."
— *Joseph Brant (Thayendanegea)*
Mohawk

Something is wrong with the white man's council. When the Micmac people used to have council, the old men would speak and tell the young men what to do — and the young men would listen and do what old men told them to. The white men have changed that, too: Now the young men speak, and the old men listen. I believe the Micmac Council was far better.

— *Peter Paul (1865)*

Why should you take by force from us that which you can obtain by love? Why should you destroy us who have provided you with food? What can you get by war?

It is better to eat good meat, be well, and sleep quietly with my women and children; to laugh and be merry with the English, and be their friend; to have copper hatchets and whatever else I want.

— *King Wahunsonacook*
Powhatan

We now crown you with the sacred emblem of the deer's antlers, the emblem of your Lordship. You shall now become a mentor of the people of the Five Nations. The thickness of your skin shall be seven spans — which is to say that you shall be filled with peace and goodwill and your mind filled with a yearning for the welfare of the people of the Confederacy.

With endless patience you shall carry out your duty, and your firmness shall be tempered with tenderness for your people. Neither anger nor fury shall lodge in your mind, and all your words and actions shall be marked with calm deliberation.

In all your deliberations in the Council, in your efforts at lawmaking, in all your official acts, self-interest shall be cast into oblivion. Cast not away the warnings of any others, if they should chide you for any error or wrong you may do, but return to the way of the Great Law, which is just and right.

Look and listen for the welfare of the whole people and have always in view not only the present but also the coming generations, even those whose faces are yet beneath the surface of the earth — the unborn of the future Nation.

— Constitution of the Five Nations

The Onondaga [Iroquois] lords shall open each council by greeting their cousin lords, and expressing their gratitude to them. And they shall offer thanks to the earth where all people dwell —

To the streams of water, the pools, the springs, and the lakes; to the maize and the fruits —

To the medicinal herbs and the trees, to the forest trees for their usefulness, to the animals that serve as food and who offer their pelts as clothing —

To the great winds and the lesser winds; to the Thunderers; and the Sun, the mighty warrior; to the moon —

To the messengers of the Great Spirit who dwells in the skies above, who gives all things useful to men, who is the source and the ruler of health and life.

Then shall the Onondaga lords declare the council open.

— Iroquois Constitution

Should any man of the Nation assist with special ability or show interest in the affairs of the Nation, if he proves himself wise, honest, and worthy of confidence, the Confederate Lords may elect him to a seat with them and he may sit in the Confederate Council. He shall be proclaimed a Pine Tree sprung up for the Nation and be installed as such at the next assembly for the installation of Lords.

Should he ever do anything contrary to the rules of the Great Peace, he may not be deposed from office — no one shall cut him down — but thereafter everyone shall be deaf to his voice and his advice. Should he resign his seat and title, no one shall prevent him. A Pine Tree Chief has no authority to name a successor, nor is his title hereditary.

— Constitution of the Five Nations

Try to do something for your people — something difficult. Have pity on your people and love them. If a man is poor, help him. Give him and his family food, give them whatever they ask for. If there is discord among your people, intercede.

Take your sacred pipe and walk into their midst. Die if necessary in your attempt to bring about reconciliation. Then, when order has been restored and they see you lying dead on the ground, still holding in your hand the sacred pipe, the symbol of peace and reconciliation, then assuredly will they know that you have been a real chief.

— Winnebago lesson

No person among us desires any other reward for performing a brave and worthy action, but the consciousness of having served his nation.

— Joseph Brant (Thayendanegea)
Mohawk

6

THE WAYS OF THE HEART

"My friends, how desperately do we need to be loved and to love."

— *Chief Dan George*

My friends, how desperately do we need to be loved and to love. When Christ said that man does not live by bread alone, he spoke of a hunger. This hunger was not the hunger of the body. It was not the hunger for bread. He spoke of a hunger that begins deep down in the very depths of our being. He spoke of a need as vital as breath. He spoke of our hunger for love.

Love is something you and I must have. We must have it because our spirit feeds upon it. We must have it because without it we become weak and faint. Without love our self-esteem weakens. Without it our

courage fails. Without love we can no longer look out confidently at the world. We turn inward and begin to feed upon our own personalities, and little by little we destroy ourselves.

With it we are creative. With it we march tirelessly. With it, and with it alone, we are able to sacrifice for others.

— *Chief Dan George*

My heart is filled with joy, when I see you here, as the brooks fill with water when the snows melt in the spring, and I feel glad, as the ponies are when the fresh grass starts in the beginning of the year.

I heard of your coming, when I was many sleeps away, and I made but few camps before I met you. I knew that you had come to do good to me and to my people. I look for the benefits, which would last forever, and so my face shines with joy, as I look upon you.

— *Ten Bears*
Yamparika Comanche

My heart laughs with joy because I am in your presence. . . . Ah, how much more beautiful is the sun today than when you were angry with us!

— Chitmachas Chief
(name unknown)

Oh, the comfort, the inexpressible comfort of feeling safe with a person, having neither to weigh thought nor measure words, but pouring them all right out, just as they are, chaff and grain together, certain that a faithful hand will take and sift them, keep what is worth keeping, and with a breath of kindness, blow the rest away.

— *Anonymous*
Shoshone

If all would talk and then do as you have done, the sun of peace would shine forever.

— *Satank*
Kiowa

Father, I love your daughter, will you give her to me, that the small roots of her heart may entangle with mine, so that the strongest wind that blows shall never separate them.

It is true I love him only, whose heart is like the sweet juice that runs from the sugar-tree and is brother to the aspen leaf, that always lives and shivers.

— *Anonymous*
Canadian

7

THE WAYS OF BELIEVING

"We do not want churches because they will teach us to quarrel about God. . . ."

— *Chief Joseph*
Nez Perce

You tell us that baptism is absolutely necessary to go to heaven. If there were a man so good that he had never offended God, and if he died without baptism, would he go to hell, never having given any offense to God? If he goes to hell, then God must not love all good people, since He throws one into the fire.

You teach us that God existed before the creation of heaven and earth. If He did, where did He live, since there was neither heaven nor earth?

You say that the angels were created in the beginning of the world, and that those who disobeyed were cast into hell. How can that be so, since you say the

angels sinned before earth's creation, and hell is in the depths of the earth?

You declare that those who go to hell do not come out of it, and yet you relate stories of the damned who have appeared in the world — how is that to be understood?

Ah, how I would like to kill devils, since they do so much harm! But if they are made like men and some are even among men, do they still feel the fire of hell? Why is it that they do not repent for having offended God? If they did repent, would not God be merciful to them? If Our Lord has suffered for all sinners, why do not they receive pardon from him?

You say that the virgin, mother of Jesus Christ, is not God, and that she has never offended God. You also say that her Son has redeemed all men, and atoned for all; but if she has done nothing wrong, her Son could not redeem her nor atone for her.

— Young "savage" seminarians, 12-15 years old,
to the Jesuit father Paul Le Jeune, late 1630s

Our wise men are called Fathers, and they truly sustain that character. Do you call yourselves Christians? Does then the religion of Him whom you call your Savior inspire your spirit, and guide your practices? Surely not.

It is recorded of him that a bruised reed he never broke. Cease, then, to call yourselves Christians, lest you declare to the world your hypocrisy. Cease, too, to call other nations savage, when you are tenfold more the children of cruelty than they.

— *Joseph Brant (Thayendanegea)*
Mohawk

We have men among us, like the whites, who pretend to know the right path, but will not consent to show it without pay! I have no faith in their paths, but believe that every man must make his own path!

— *Black Hawk*
Sauk

We do not want churches because they will teach us to quarrel about God, as the Catholics and Protestants do. We do not want to learn that.

We may quarrel with men sometimes about things on this earth. But we never quarrel about God. We do not want to learn that.

— *Chief Joseph*
Nez Perce

I think that wherever the Great Spirit places his people, they ought to be satisfied to remain, and thankful for what He has given them, and not drive others from the country He has given them because it happens to be better than theirs!

This is contrary to our way of thinking; and from my intercourse with the whites, I have learned that one great principle of their religion is "to do unto others as you wish them to do unto you!" The settlers on our frontiers and on our lands never seem to think of it, if we are to judge by their actions.

For my part, I am of the opinion that so far as we have reason, we have a right to use it in determining what is right or wrong, and we should pursue that path we believe to be right.

If the Great and Good Spirit wished us to believe and to do as the whites, he could easily change our opinions, so that we would see, and think, and act as they do. We are nothing compared to His power, and we feel and know it.

— *Black Hawk*
Sauk

From Wakan Tanka, the Great Spirit, there came a great unifying life force that flowed in and through all things — the flowers of the plains, blowing winds, rocks, trees, birds, animals — and was the same force that had been breathed into the first man. Thus all things were kindred, and were brought together by the same Great Mystery.

Kinship with all creatures of the earth, sky, and water was a real and active principle. In the animal and bird world there existed a brotherly feeling that kept the Lakota safe among them. And so close did some of the Lakotas come to their feathered and furred friends that in true brotherhood they spoke a common tongue.

The animals had rights — the right of man's protection, the right to live, the right to multiply, the right to freedom, and the right to man's indebtedness — and in recognition of these rights the Lakota never enslaved an animal, and spared all life that was not needed for food and clothing.

This concept of life and its relations was humanizing, and gave to the Lakota an abiding love. It filled his being with the joy and mystery of living; it gave him reverence for all life; it made a place for all things in the scheme of existence with equal importance to all.

The Lakota could despise no creature, for all were of one blood, made by the same hand, and filled with the essence of the Great Mystery. In spirit, the Lakota were humble and meek. "Blessed are the meek, for they shall inherit the earth" — this was true for the Lakota, and from the earth they inherited secrets long since forgotten. Their religion was sane, natural, and human.

— *Chief Luther Standing Bear*
Teton Sioux

Grandfather, Great Spirit, once more behold me on earth and lean to hear my feeble voice. You lived first, and you are older than all need, older than all prayer. All things belong to you — the two-legged, the four-legged, the wings of the air, and all green things that live.

You have set the powers of the four quarters of the earth to cross each other. You have made me cross the good road, and the road of difficulties, and where they cross, the place is holy. Day in, day out, forevermore, you are the life of things.

— *Black Elk*
Oglala Sioux

8

THE BETRAYAL OF THE LAND

"Sell a country! Why not sell the air, the great sea, as well as the earth?"

— *Tecumseh*
Shawnee

Nothing the Great Mystery placed in the land of the Indian pleased the white man, and nothing escaped his transforming hand. Wherever forests have not been mowed down, wherever the animal is recessed in their quiet protection, wherever the earth is not bereft of four-footed life — that to him is an "unbroken wilderness."

But, because for the Lakota there was no wilderness, because nature was not dangerous but hospitable, not forbidding but friendly, Lakota philosophy was healthy — free from fear and dogmatism. And here I find the great distinction between the faith of the

Indian and the white man. Indian faith sought the harmony of man with his surroundings; the other sought the dominance of surroundings.

In sharing, in loving all and everything, one people naturally found a due portion of the thing they sought, while, in fearing, the other found need of conquest.

For one man the world was full of beauty; for the other it was a place of sin and ugliness to be endured until he went to another world, there to become a creature of wings, half-man and half-bird.

Forever one man directed his Mystery to change the world He had made; forever this man pleaded with Him to chastise his wicked ones; and forever he implored his God to send His light to earth. Small wonder this man could not understand the other.

But the old Lakota was wise. He knew that man's heart, away from nature, becomes hard; he knew that lack of respect for growing, living things soon led to lack of respect for humans, too. So he kept his children close to nature's softening influence.

— *Chief Luther Standing Bear*
Oglala Sioux

Some of our chiefs make the claim that the land belongs to us. It is not what the Great Spirit told me. He told me that the lands belong to Him, that no people owns the land; that I was not to forget to tell this to the white people when I met them in council.

— *Kanekuk*
Kickapoo prophet

No tribe has the right to sell, even to each other, much less to strangers. . . . Sell a country! Why not sell the air, the great sea, as well as the earth? Didn't the Great Spirit make them all for the use of his children?

— *Tecumseh*
Shawnee

This is what was spoken by my great-grandfather at the house he made for us. . . . And these are the words that were given him by the Master of Life: "At some time there shall come among you a stranger, speaking a language you do not understand. He will try to buy the land from you, but do not sell it; keep it for an inheritance to your children."

— *Aseenewub*
Red Lake Ojibwe

My reason teaches me that land cannot be sold. The Great Spirit gave it to his children to live upon and cultivate as far as necessary for their subsistence, and so long as they occupy and cultivate it they have the right to the soil, but if they voluntarily leave it then any other people have a right to settle on it. Nothing can be sold, except things that can be carried away.

— *Black Hawk*
Sauk

Suppose a white man should come to me and say, "Joseph, I like your horses. I want to buy them."

I say to him, "No, my horses suit me; I will not sell them."

Then he goes to my neighbor and says to him, "Joseph has some good horses. I want to buy them, but he refuses to sell."

My neighbor answers, "Pay me the money and I will sell you Joseph's horses."

The white man returns to me and says, "Joseph, I have bought your horses and you must let me have them."

If we sold our lands to the government, this is the way they bought them.

— *Chief Joseph*
Nez Perce

We know our lands have now become more valuable. The white people think we do not know their value; but we know that the land is everlasting, and the few goods we receive for it are soon worn out and gone.

> — *Canassatego*
> Treaty negotiations with Six Nations

On this land there is a great deal of timber, pine and oak, that are of much use to the white man. They send it to foreign countries, and it brings them a great deal of money.

On the land there is much grass for cattle and horses, and much good food for hogs.

On this land there is a great deal of tobacco raised, which likewise brings much money. Even the streams are valuable to the white man, to grind the wheat and corn that grows on this land. The pine trees that are dead are valuable for tar.

All these things are lasting benefits. But if the Indians are given just a few goods for their lands, in one or two seasons those goods are all rotted and gone for nothing.

We are told that our lands are of no service to us; but still, if we hold our lands, there will always be a turkey, or a deer, or a fish in the streams for those young who will come after us.

We are afraid if we part with any more of our

lands the white people will not let us keep as much as will be sufficient to bury our dead.

— *Doublehead*
Creek Chief

My friends, when I went to Washington I went into your money-house and I had some young men with me, but none of us took any money out of that house. At the same time, when your Great Father's people come into my country, they go into my money-house and take money out.

— *Long Mandan*
Sioux

In early life, I was deeply hurt as I witnessed the grand old forests of Michigan, under whose shades my fore-fathers lived and died, falling before the cyclone of civilization as before a prairie fire.

In those days, I traveled thousands of miles along our winding trails, through the unbroken solitudes of the wild forest, listening to the songs of the woodland birds as they poured forth their melodies from the thick foliage above and about me.

Very seldom now do I catch one familiar note from these early warblers of the woods. They have all passed away. . . .

I now listen to the songs of other birds that have

come with the advance of civilization . . . and, like the wildwood birds our fathers used to hold their breath to hear, they sing in concert, without pride, without envy, without jealousy — alike in forest and field, alike before wigwam or castle, alike before savage or sage, alike for chief or king.

— Simon Pokagon
Potawatomi Chief

We know that the white man does not understand our ways. One portion of the land is the same to him as the next, for he is a stranger who comes in the night and takes from the land whatever he needs. The earth is not his brother, but his enemy — and when he has conquered it, he moves on. He leaves his fathers' graves, and his children's birthright is forgotten.

— Chief Seattle
Suqwamish and Duwamish

9

THE WAYS OF DYING

"Death will come, always out of season."

— *Big Elk*
Omaha Chief

I was born upon the prairie where the wind blew free and there was nothing to break the light of the sun. I was born where there were no enclosures and where everything drew a free breath.

I want to die there, and not within walls.

— *Ten Bears*
Yamparika Comanche

When an infant dies before its fourth day of life, mourning shall continue only five days.

Then shall you gather the little boys and girls at the house of mourning, and at the funeral feast a speaker

shall address the children and bid them be happy once more, even though by a death, gloom has been cast over them.

Then shall the black clouds roll away and the sky shall show blue once more. Then shall the children be again in sunshine.

— Constitution of the Five Nations

If my warriors are to fight they are too few; if they are to die they are too many.

— *Hendrick*
Mohawk

What! Would you wish that there should be no dried trees in the woods and no dead branches on a tree that is growing old?

— A seventy-year-old Huron

Do not grieve. Misfortunes will happen to the wisest and best of men. Death will come, always out of season. It is the command of the Great Spirit, and all nations and people must obey. What is past and what cannot be prevented should not be grieved for. . . . Misfortunes do not flourish particularly in our lives — they grow everywhere.

— *Big Elk*
Omaha Chief

Old age was simply a delightful time, when the old people sat on the sunny doorsteps, playing in the sun with the children, until they fell asleep. At last, they failed to wake up.

— *James Paytiamo*
Acoma Pueblo

10

THE PASSING OF THE WAYS

"Our Indian life, I know, is gone forever."
— *Waheenee*
Hidatsa (North Dakota)

When I was a boy, the Sioux owned the world. The sun rose and set on their land; they sent ten thousand men to battle.

Where are the warriors today? Who slew them? Where are our lands? Who owns them?

What white man can say I ever stole his land or a penny of his money? Yet they say I am a thief.

What white woman, however lonely, was ever captive or insulted by me? Yet they say I am a bad Indian.

What white man has ever seen me drunk? Who has ever come to me hungry and left me unfed? Who has ever seen me beat my wives or abuse my children?

What law have I broken?

Is it wrong for me to love my own? Is it wicked for me because my skin is red? Because I am a Sioux? Because I was born where my father lived? Because I would die for my people and my country?

— *Sitting Bull*
Teton Sioux

The ground on which we stand is sacred ground. It is the dust and blood of our ancestors. On these plains the Great White Father in Washington sent his soldiers armed with long knives and rifles to slay the Indian. Many of them sleep on yonder hill where Pahaska — White Chief of the Long Hair [General Custer] — so bravely fought and fell.

A few more passing suns will see us here no more, and our dust and bones will mingle with these same prairies. I see as in a vision of the dying spark of our council fires, the ashes cold and white. I see no longer the curling smoke rising from our lodge poles. I hear no longer the songs of the women as they prepare the meal.

The antelope have gone; the buffalo wallows are empty. Only the wail of the coyote is heard. The white man's medicine is stronger than ours; his iron horse [the railroad] rushes over the buffalo trail. He talks to us through his "whispering spirit" [the telephone].

We are like birds with a broken wing. My heart is cold within me. My eyes are growing dim — I am old.

— Chief Plenty Coups
Crow

When the buffalo went away the hearts of my people fell to the ground, and they could not lift them up again.

After this nothing happened. There was little singing anywhere.

— Chief Plenty Coups
Crow

I remember the old men of my village. These old, old men used to prophesy about the coming of the white man. They would go about tapping their canes on the adobe floor of the house, and call to us children.

"Listen! Listen! The gray-eyed people are coming nearer and nearer. They are building an iron road. They are coming nearer every day. There will be a time when you will mix with these people. That is when the Gray Eyes are going to get you to drink hot, black water, which you will drink whenever you eat. Then your teeth will become soft.

"They will get you to smoke at a young age, so that your eyes will run tears on windy days, and your eyesight will be poor. Your joints will crack when you want to move slowly and softly.

"You will sleep on soft beds and will not like to rise early. When you begin to wear heavy clothes and sleep under heavy covers, then you will grow lazy. Then there will be no more singing heard in the valleys as you walk.

"When you begin to eat with iron sticks, your tones will grow louder. You will speak louder and talk over your parents. You will grow disobedient. You will mix with those gray-eyed people, and you will learn their ways; you will break up your homes, and murder and steal."

Such things have come true, and I have to compare my generation with the old generation. We are not as good as they were; we are not as healthy as they were.

How did these old men know what was coming? That is what I would like to know.

—*James Paytiamo*
Acoma Pueblo

I am an old woman now. The buffaloes and black-tail deer are gone, and our Indian ways are almost gone. Sometimes I find it hard to believe that I ever lived them.

My little son grew up in the white man's school. He can read books, and he owns cattle and has a farm. He is a leader among our Hidatsa people, helping teach them to follow the white man's road.

He is kind to me. We no longer live in an earth lodge, but in a house with chimneys, and my son's wife cooks by a stove.

But for me, I cannot forget our old ways.

Often in summer I rise at daybreak and steal out to the corn fields, and as I hoe the corn I sing to it, as we did when I was young. No one cares for our corn songs now.

Sometimes in the evening I sit, looking out on the big Missouri. The sun sets, and dusk steals over the water. In the shadows I seem again to see our Indian village, with smoke curling upward from the earth lodges, and in the river's roar I hear the yells of the warriors, and the laughter of little children as of old.

It is but an old woman's dream. Then I see but shadows and hear only the roar of the river, and tears come into my eyes. Our Indian life, I know, is gone forever.

— *Waheenee*
Hidatsa (North Dakota)

11

THE WAYS OF THE WHITE MAN

*"What do we know of the manner of the laws
and customs of the white people?"*

— *Black Hawk*
Sauk

Many of the white man's ways are past our understanding. . . . They put a great store upon writing; there is always paper.

The white people must think that paper has some mysterious power to help them in the world. The Indian needs no writings; words that are true sink deep into his heart, where they remain. He never forgets them. On the other hand, if the white man loses his papers, he is helpless.

I once heard one of their preachers say that no white man was admitted to heaven unless there were writings about him in a great book!

— *Four Guns*
Oglala Sioux

I am truly astonished that the French have so little cleverness. They try to persuade us to convert our poles, our barks, and our wigwams into their houses of stone and of wood that are as tall and lofty as these trees. Very well! But why do men of five to six feet in height need houses that are sixty to eighty?

Do we not have all the advantages in our houses that you have in yours, such as reposing, drinking, sleeping, eating, and amusing ourselves with our friends when we wish?

Have you as much ingenuity as the Indians, who carry their houses and their wigwams with them so that they may lodge wherever they please? We can say that we are at home everywhere, because we set up our wigwams with ease wherever we go, without asking permission from anyone.

You reproach us — very inappropriately — and tell us that our country is a little hell in contrast with France, which you compare to a terrestrial paradise. If this is true, why did you leave it? Why did you abandon your wives, children, relatives, and friends?

Which of these is the wisest and happiest — he who labors without ceasing and only obtains, with great trouble, enough to live on, or he who rests in comfort and finds all that he needs in the pleasure of hunting and fishing?

Learn now, my brother, once and for all, because I

must open my heart to you: There is no Indian who does not consider himself infinitely more happy and more powerful than the French.

— Micmac Chief (1676)

The English, in general, are a noble, generous-minded people, free to act and free to think. They very much pride themselves on their civil and religious privileges; on their learning, generosity, manufacturing, and commerce; and they think that no other nation is equal to them. . . .

No nation, I think, can be more fond of novelties than the English; they gaze upon foreigners as if they had just dropped down from the moon. . . .

They are truly industrious, and in general very honest and upright. But their close attention to business produces, I think, too much worldly-mindedness, and hence they forget to think enough about their souls and their God.

Their motto seems to be "Money, money, get money, get rich, and be a gentleman." With this sentiment, they fly about in every direction, like a swarm of bees, in search of the treasure that lies so near their hearts.

— *Peter Jones, or Kahkewaquonaby*
("Sacred Waving Fathers")
Ojibwe

Once I was in Victoria, and I saw a very large house. They told me it was a bank, and that the white men place their money there to be taken care of, and that by and by they got it back, with interest.

We are Indians, and we have no such bank; but when we have plenty of money or blankets, we give them away to other chiefs and people, and by and by they return them, with interest, and our hearts feel good. Our way of giving is our bank.

— *Maquinna*
Nootka Chief

Strong liquor was first sold to us by the Dutch, and they were blind, they had no eyes, they could not see how much it hurt us. The next people who came were the Swedes, who continued to sell us strong liquor. We love it, so we cannot refuse it.

It makes us wild; we do not know what we are doing. We abuse one another; we throw one another into the fire. . . .

Through drinking, seven score of our people have been killed. The cask must be sealed, it must be made fast; it must not leak by day or night, in the light or in the dark.

— *Okanicon*
Delaware

The Americans have been very kind to us; they are not as arrogant as the English, but very persevering in all their ways.

They pay more respect to their women than the English, and they see the things that belong to others without bitterness, or regret. The working classes of the English call their rich men "Big Bugs," but the Yankees call them "Top Notches."

The Yankees put their feet upon the tables, chairs, or chimney pieces when smoking their cigars or reading their newspapers. They are not as much slaves to their civilization as the English; they like to be comfortable, something like ourselves, placing one leg upon the other knee while basking ourselves in the sun.

A real comfort is better than an artificial one to the human nature.

> — *George Henry*
> *Maungwudaus ("Big Legging")*
> Ojibwe Methodist preacher

I have attended dinners among white people. Their ways are not our ways.

We eat in silence, quietly smoke a pipe, and depart. Thus is our host honored.

This is not the way of the white man. After his food

has been eaten, one is expected to say foolish things. Then the host feels honored.

— *Four Guns*
Oglala Sioux

They are a heartless nation, that is certain. They have made some of their people servants — yes, slaves! We have never believed in keeping slaves, but it seems that the white people do! It is our belief that they painted their servants black a long time ago, to tell them from the rest — and now the slaves have children born to them of the same color!

The greatest object of their lives seems to be to acquire possessions — to be rich. They desire to possess the whole world.

For thirty years they tried to entice us to sell our land to them. Finally, their soldiers took it by force, and we have been driven away from our beautiful country.

They are indeed an extraordinary people. They have divided the day into hours, like the moons of the year. In fact, they measure everything. Not one of them would let so much as a turnip go from his field unless he received full value for it. I understand that sometimes their great men make a feast and invite many, but when it is over, the guests are required to pay for what they have eaten before leaving the house. . . .

I am also told, but this I hardly believe, that their Great Chief compels every man to pay him for the land he lives upon and all his personal goods — even those he needs for his own existence — every year. I am sure we could not live under such a law.

In war they have leaders and war-chiefs of different grades. The common warriors are driven forward like a herd of antelopes to face the foe. It is because of this manner of fighting — from compulsion and not from personal bravery — that we count no coup on them. A lone warrior can do much harm to a large army of them — especially when they are in unfamiliar territory.

> — *Charles Alexander Eastman's uncle*
> Santee Sioux

The white man who is our agent is so stingy that he carries a linen rag in his pocket into which to blow his nose, for fear he might blow away something of value.

> — *Piapot*
> Cree Chief

I have carried a heavy load on my back ever since I was a boy. I realized then that we could not hold our own with the white men. We were like deer. They were like grizzly bears. We had a small country. Their country was large. We were contented to let things remain as the Great Spirit Chief made them. They were not, and would change the rivers and mountains if they did not suit them.

— *Chief Joseph*
Nez Perce

Here, for the first time, I touched the goose quill to the treaty — not knowing, however, that by that act I consented to give away my village! Had that been explained to me, I should have opposed it, and never would have signed their treaty, as my recent conduct has clearly proven.

What do we know of the manner of the laws and customs of the white people? They might buy our bodies for dissection, and we would touch the goose quill to confirm it, without knowing what we were doing. This was the case with myself and my people in touching the goose quill the first time.

We can only judge what is proper and right by our standard of right and wrong, which differs widely from the whites, if I have been correctly informed. The whites may do bad all their lives, and then, if they are sorry for it when they are about to die, all is well!

But with us it is different: We must continue throughout our lives to do what we conceive to be good. If we have corn and meat, and know of a family that has none, we divide with them. If we have more blankets than are sufficient, and others have not enough, we must give to them that want.

— *Black Hawk*
Sauk

Brothers, money to us is of no value, and to most of us unknown; and as no consideration whatever can induce us to sell the lands, on which we get sustenance for our women and children, we hope we may be allowed to point out a mode by which your settlers may be easily removed and peace obtained.

Brothers, we know that these settlers are poor, or they would never have ventured to live in a country that has been in continual trouble ever since they crossed the Ohio. Divide therefore this large sum of money that you have offered to us among these people . . . and we are persuaded they would most readily accept it in lieu of the lands you sold to them. . . .

— *Letter (1793)*
The Seven Nations of Canada

Tell your people that since the Great Father promised that we should never be removed we have been moved five times. I think you had better put the Indians on wheels so you can run them about wherever you wish.

— Anonymous Chief (1876)

I know that robes, leggings, moccasins, bear claws, and so on are of little value to you, but we wish you to have them and to preserve them in some conspicuous part of your lodge, so that when we are gone and the sod turned over our bones, if our children should visit this place, as we do now, they may see and recognize with pleasure the things of their fathers, and reflect on the times that are past.

— *Sharitarish*
Pawnee

I will follow the white man's trail. I will make him my friend, but I will not bend my back to his burdens. I will be cunning as a coyote. I will ask him to help me understand his ways, then I will prepare the way for my children. Maybe they will outrun the white man in his own shoes.

There are but two ways for us. One leads to hunger and death, the other leads to where the poor white man lives. Beyond is the happy hunting ground where the white man cannot go.

— *Many Horses*
Oglala Sioux

12

THE WAYS OF CIVILIZATION

"Civilization has been thrust upon me . . . and it has not added one whit to my love for truth, honesty, and generosity. . . ."

— *Chief Luther Standing Bear*
Oglala Sioux

Much has been said of the want of what you term "civilization" among the Indians. Many proposals have been made to us to adopt your laws, your religion, your manners, and your customs. We do not see the propriety of such a reformation.

We should be better pleased if we could actually see the good effects of these doctrines in your own practices rather than hearing you talk about them, or reading your newspapers on such subjects.

You say, for example, "Why do not the Indians till the ground and live as we do?" May we not ask with

equal propriety, "Why do not the white people hunt and live as we do?"

— *Old Tassel*
Cherokee

The more I consider the condition of the white men, the more fixed becomes my opinion that, instead of gaining, they have lost much by subjecting themselves to what they call the laws and regulations of civilized societies.

— *Tomochichi*
Creek Chief

In the government you call civilized, the happiness of the people is constantly sacrificed to the splendor of empire. Hence the origin of your codes of criminal and civil laws; hence your dungeons and prisons. We have no prisons; we have no pompous parade of courts; we have no written laws; and yet judges are as highly revered among us as they are among you, and their decisions are as much regarded.

We have among us no exalted villains above the control of our laws. Daring wickedness is here never allowed to triumph over helpless innocence. The estates of widows and orphans are never devoured by enterprising swindlers.

We have no robbery under the pretext of law.

— Joseph Brant (Thayendanegea)
Mohawk

The white man's police have protected us only as well as the feathers of a bird protect it from the frosts of winter.

— Crowfoot
Blackfeet Chief

The sight of your cities pains the eyes of the red man. But perhaps it is because the red man is a savage and does not understand.

There is no quiet place in the white man's cities, no place to hear the leaves of spring or the rustle of insects' wings. Perhaps it is because I am a savage and do not understand, but the clatter only seems to insult the ears.

The Indian prefers the soft sound of the wind darting over the face of the pond, the smell of the wind itself cleansed by a midday rain, or scented with piñon pine. The air is precious to the red man, for all things share the same breath — the animals, the trees, the man.

Like a man who has been dying for many days, a man in your city is numb to the stench.

— *Chief Seattle*
Suqwamish and Duwamish

The Great Spirit has given the white man great fore-sightedness; he sees everything at a distance, and his mind invents and makes the most extraordinary things. But the red man has been made shortsighted. He sees only what is close around him and knows nothing except what his father knew. . . .

— *Crow Belly*
Gros Ventre Chief

The attempted transformation of the Indian by the white man and the chaos that has resulted are but the fruits of the white man's disobedience of a fundamental and spiritual law.

"Civilization" has been thrust upon me since the days of the reservations, and it has not added one whit to my sense of justice, to my reverence for the rights of life, to my love for truth, honesty, and generosity, or to my faith in Wakan Tanka, God of the Lakotas.

For after all the great religions have been preached and expounded, or have been revealed by brilliant scholars, or have been written in fine books and embellished in fine language with finer covers, man — all man — is still confronted with the Great Mystery.

— *Chief Luther Standing Bear*
Oglala Sioux

White man's pictures all fade, but the Indian's memories last forever.

— Indian guide to Tom Wilson (1882)

13

HEED THESE WORDS

"Continue to contaminate your own bed, and you will one night suffocate in your own waste."
— *Chief Seattle*
Suqwamish and Duwamish

The white man does not understand America. He is too far removed from its formative processes. The roots of the tree of his life have not yet grasped the rock and the soil.

The white man is still troubled by primitive fears; he still has in his consciousness the perils of this frontier continent, some of it not yet having yielded to his questing footsteps and inquiring eyes.

He shudders still with the memory of the loss of his forefathers upon its scorching deserts and forbidding mountaintops. The man from Europe is still a foreigner and an alien. And he still hates the man who

questioned his path across the continent.

But in the Indian the spirit of the land is still vested; it will be a long time until other men are able to divine and meet its rhythm. Men must be born and reborn to belong. Their bodies must be formed of the dust of their forefathers' bones.

— *Chief Luther Standing Bear*
Oglala Sioux

A few more hours, a few more winters, and none of the children of the great tribes that once lived on this earth, or that roamed in small bands in the woods, will be left to mourn the graves of a people once as powerful and hopeful as yours.

The whites, too, shall pass — perhaps sooner than other tribes. Continue to contaminate your own bed, and you will one night suffocate in your own waste.

When the buffalo are all slaughtered, the wild horses all tamed, the secret corners of the forest heavy with the scent of many men, and the view of the ripe hills blotted by talking wires, where is the thicket? Gone. Where is the eagle? Gone.

And what is to say farewell to the swift and the hunt, to the end of living and the beginning of survival? We might understand if we knew what it was that the white man dreams, what he describes to his children on the long winter nights, what visions he burns into their minds, so they will wish for tomorrow. But we are savages. The white man's dreams are hidden from us.

— Chief Seattle
Suqwamish and Duwamish

If the Great Spirit had desired me to be a white man he would have made me so in the first place. He put in your heart certain wishes and plans; in my heart he put other and different desires.

Each man is good in the sight of the Great Spirit. It is not necessary for eagles to be crows. Now we are poor but we are free. No white man controls our footsteps. If we must die, we die defending our rights.

— Sitting Bull
Teton Sioux

The white people think we have no brains in our heads. They are great and powerful, and that makes them make war with us. We are but a little handful to what you are.

But remember . . . when you hunt for a rattlesnake, you usually cannot find it — and perhaps it will bite you before you see it.

— Shingis
Delaware Chief

The red man has ever fled the approach of the white man, as the morning mist flees before the morning sun. . . . It matters little where we pass the remnants of our days. They will not be many.

But why should I mourn the untimely fate of my people? Your time of decay may be distant, but it will surely come, for even the white man, whose God walked and talked with him as friend with friend, cannot be exempt from the common destiny. We may be brothers, after all. We will see. . . .

— *Chief Seattle*
Suqwamish and Duwamish

Can we talk of integration until there is integration of hearts and minds? Unless you have this, you have only a physical presence, and the walls between us are as high as the mountain range.

— *Chief Dan George*

The color of the skin makes no difference. What is good and just for one is good and just for the other, and the Great Spirit made all men brothers.

I have red skin, but my grandfather was a white man. What does it matter? It is not the color of the skin that makes me good or bad.

— *White Shield*
Arikara Chief

The path to glory is rough, and many gloomy hours obscure it. May the Great Spirit shed light on your path, so that you may never experience the humility that the power of the American government has reduced me to. This is the wish of a man who, in his native forests, was once as proud and bold as yourself.

— *Black Hawk*
Sauk

"When you see a new trail, or a footprint you do not know, follow it to the point of knowing."

— *Uncheedah*
The grandmother of Ohiyesa

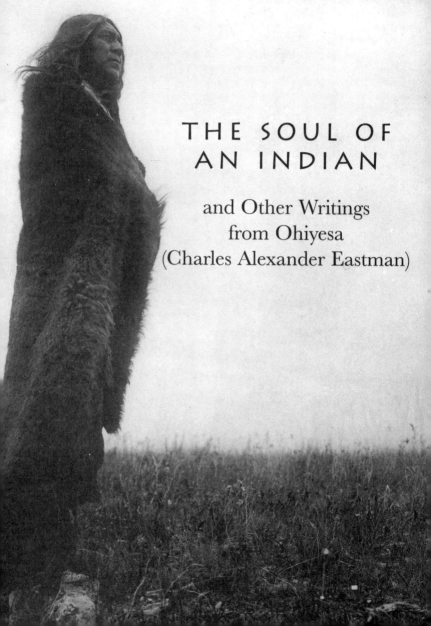

PART 2

THE SOUL OF
AN INDIAN

and Other Writings
from Ohiyesa
(Charles Alexander Eastman)

14

FOREWORD

"We also have a religion which has been given to our forefathers, and has been handed down to us their children. It teaches us to be thankful, to be united, and to love one another! We never quarrel about religion."

Thus spoke the great Seneca orator, Red Jacket, in his superb reply to Missionary Cram more than a century ago, and I have often heard the same thought expressed by my countrymen.

I have attempted to paint the religious life of the typical American Indian as it was before we knew the white race. I have long wished to do this, because I cannot find that it has ever been seriously, adequately, and

sincerely done. Our religion is the last thing about us that the person of another race will ever understand.

First, we Indians do not speak of these deep matters so long as we believe in them, and those of us who have ceased to believe speak inaccurately and slightingly.

Second, even if we can be induced to speak, the racial and religious prejudice of the other stands in the way of any sympathetic comprehension.

Third, practically all existing studies on this subject have been made during the transition period, when the original beliefs and philosophy of the Native American were already undergoing rapid disintegration.

There are to be found here and there superficial accounts of strange customs and ceremonies, of which the symbolism or inner meaning was largely hidden from the observer; and there has been a great deal of material collected in recent years which is without value because it is modern and hybrid, inextricably mixed with Biblical legend and Caucasian philosophy. Some of it has even been invented for commercial purposes. Find an Indian who is more concerned with profit than his heritage, and he will possibly provide you with sacred songs, a mythology, and folklore to order!

My writings do not pretend to be a scientific treatise. They are as true as I can make them to my childhood teaching and ancestral ideals, but from the human, not the ethnological standpoint. I have not cared to pile up more dry bones, but to clothe them with flesh and blood. So much that has been written by strangers of our ancient faith and worship treats it mainly as a matter of curiosity. I should like to emphasize its universal quality, its personal appeal!

The first missionaries who came among us were good men, but they were imbued with the narrowness of their age. They branded us as pagans and devil-worshipers, and demanded that we renounce our gods as false. They even told us that we were eternally lost unless we adopted their faith and all its symbols.

We of the twentieth century know better. We know that all religious aspiration, all sincere worship, can have but one source and goal. We know that the God of the educated and the God of the child, the God of the civilized and the God of the primitive, is after all the same God; and that this God does not measure our differences, but embraces all who live rightly and humbly on the earth.

— *Ohiyesa (Charles Alexander Eastman)*

15

THE WAYS OF THE SPIRIT

Is there not something worthy of perpetuation in our Indian spirit of democracy, where Earth, our mother, was free to all, and no one sought to impoverish or enslave his neighbor?

— *Ohiyesa*

We do not chart and measure the vast field of nature or express her wonders in the terms of science; on the contrary, we see miracles on every hand — the miracle of life in seed and egg, the miracle of death in a lightning flash and in the swelling deep!

THE GREAT MYSTERY

The attitude of the American Indian toward the Eternal, the Great Mystery that surrounds and embraces us, is as simple as it is exalted. To us it is the supreme conception, bringing with it the fullest measure of joy and satisfaction possible in this life.

The worship of the Great Mystery is silent, solitary, free from all self-seeking.

It is silent, because all speech is of necessity feeble and imperfect; therefore the souls of our ancestors ascended to God in wordless adoration.

It is solitary, because we believe that God is nearer to us in solitude, and there are no priests authorized to come between us and our Maker. None can exhort or confess or in any way meddle with the religious experience of another. All of us are created children of God, and all stand erect, conscious of our divinity. Our faith cannot be formulated in creeds, nor forced upon any who are unwilling to receive it; hence there is no preaching, proselytizing, nor persecution, neither are there any scoffers or atheists.

Our religion is an attitude of mind, not a dogma.

THE TEMPLE OF NATURE

There are no temples or shrines among us save those of nature. Being children of nature, we are intensely poetical. We would deem it sacrilege to build a house for The One who may be met face to face in the mysterious, shadowy aisles of the primeval forest, or on the sunlit bosom of virgin prairies, upon dizzy spires and pinnacles of naked rock, and in the vast jeweled vault of the night sky! A God who is enrobed in filmy veils of cloud, there on the rim of the visible world where our Great-Grandfather Sun kindles his evening camp-fire;

who rides upon the rigorous wind of the north, or breathes forth spirit upon fragrant southern airs, whose war canoe is launched upon majestic rivers and inland seas — such a God needs no lesser cathedral.

THE POWER OF SILENCE

We first Americans mingle with our pride an exceptional humility. Spiritual arrogance is foreign to our nature and teaching. We never claimed that the power of articulate speech is proof of superiority over "dumb creation"; on the other hand, it is to us a perilous gift.

We believe profoundly in silence — the sign of a perfect equilibrium. Silence is the absolute poise or balance of body, mind, and spirit. Those who can preserve their selfhood ever calm and unshaken by the storms of existence — not a leaf, as it were, astir on the tree; not a ripple upon the shining pool — those, in the mind of the person of nature, possess the ideal attitude and conduct of life.

If you ask us, "What is silence?" we will answer, "It is the Great Mystery. The holy silence is God's voice."

If you ask, "What are the fruits of silence?" we will answer, "They are self-control, true courage or endurance, patience, dignity, and reverence. Silence is the cornerstone of character."

"Guard your tongue in youth," said the old chief, Wabasha, "and in age you may mature a thought that will be of service to your people."

THE PRESENCE OF SPIRIT

Naturally magnanimous and open-minded, we have always preferred to believe that the Spirit of God is not breathed into humans alone, but that the whole created universe shares in the immortal perfection of its Maker.

The elements and majestic forces in nature — lightning, wind, water, fire, and frost — are regarded with awe as spiritual powers, but always secondary and intermediate in character. We believe that the spirit pervades all creation and that every creature possesses a soul in some degree, though not necessarily a soul conscious of itself. The tree, the waterfall, the grizzly bear, each is an embodied Force, and as such an object of reverence.

We Indians love to come into sympathy and spiritual communion with our brothers and sisters of the animal kingdom, whose inarticulate souls hold for us something of the sinless purity that we attribute to the innocent and irresponsible child. We have a faith in their instincts, as in a mysterious wisdom given from above; and while we humbly accept the sacrifice of their bodies to preserve our own, we pay homage to their spirits in prescribed prayers and offerings.

POVERTY AND SIMPLICITY

We original Americans have generally been despised by our white conquerors for our poverty and simplicity.

They forget, perhaps, that our religion forbade the accumulation of wealth and the enjoyment of luxury. To us, as to other spiritually-minded people in every age and race, the love of possessions is a snare, and the burdens of a complex society a source of needless peril and temptation.

It is simple truth that we Indians did not, so long as our native philosophy held sway over our minds, either envy or desire to imitate the splendid achievements of the white race. In our own thought we rose superior to them! We scorned them, even as a lofty spirit absorbed in its own task rejects the soft beds, the luxurious food, the pleasure-worshipping dalliance of a rich neighbor. It was clear to us that virtue and happiness are independent of these things, if not incompatible with them.

Furthermore, it was the rule of our life to share the fruits of our skill and success with our less fortunate brothers and sisters. Thus we kept our spirits free from the clog of pride, avarice, or envy, and carried out, as we believed, the divine decree — a matter profoundly important to us.

NATURE AND SOLITUDE

As children of nature, we have always looked upon the concentration of population as the prolific mother of all evils, moral no less than physical. It was not, then, wholly from ignorance or improvidence that we failed to establish permanent towns and to develop a material civilization. We have always believed that food is good, while surfeit kills; that love is good, but lust destroys; and not less dreaded than the pestilence following upon crowded and unsanitary dwellings is the loss of spiritual power inseparable from too close contact with one's fellow men.

All who have lived much out of doors, whether Indian or otherwise, know that there is a magnetic and powerful force that accumulates in solitude but is quickly dissipated by life in a crowd. Even our enemies have recognized that for a certain innate power and self-poise, wholly independent of circumstances, the American Indian is unsurpassed among the races.

THE IMPORTANCE OF PRAYER

Prayer — the daily recognition of the Unseen and the Eternal — is our one inevitable duty.

We Indian people have traditionally divided mind into two parts — the spiritual mind and the physical mind. The first — the spiritual mind — is concerned only with the essence of things, and it is this we seek to strengthen by spiritual prayer, during which the body is subdued by fasting and hardship. In this type of prayer there is no beseeching of favor or help.

The second, or physical, mind, is lower. It is concerned with all personal or selfish matters, like success in hunting or warfare, relief from sickness, or the sparing of a beloved life. All ceremonies, charms, or incantations designed to secure a benefit or to avert a danger are recognized as emanating from the physical self.

The rites of this physical worship are wholly symbolic; we may have sundances and other ceremonies, but the Indian no more worships the sun than the Christian worships the cross. In our view, the Sun and the Earth are the parents of all organic life. And, it must be admitted, in this our thinking is scientific truth as well as poetic metaphor.

For the Sun, as the universal father, sparks the principle of growth in nature, and in the patient and fruitful womb of our mother, the Earth, are hidden embryos of plants and men. Therefore our reverence and love for the Sun and the Earth are really an imaginative extension of our love for our immediate parents, and with this feeling of filial devotion is joined a willingness to appeal to them for such good gifts as we may desire. This is the material or physical prayer.

But, in a broader sense, our whole life is prayer because every act of our life is, in a very real sense, a religious act. Our daily devotions are more important to us than food.

We wake at daybreak, put on our moccasins and step down to the water's edge. Here we throw handfuls of clear, cold water into our face, or plunge in bodily.

After the bath, we stand erect before the advancing dawn, facing the sun as it dances upon the horizon, and offer our unspoken prayer. Our mate may proceed or follow us in our devotions, but never accompanies us. Each soul must meet the morning sun, the new sweet earth, and the Great Silence alone.

Whenever, in the course of our day, we might come upon a scene that is strikingly beautiful or sublime — the black thundercloud with the rainbow's glowing arch above the mountain; a white waterfall in the heart of a green gorge; a vast prairie tinged with the blood-red of sunset — we pause for an instant in the attitude of worship.

We recognize the spirit in all creation, and believe that we draw spiritual power from it. Our respect for the immortal part of our brothers and sisters, the animals, often leads us so far as to lay out the body of any game we catch and decorate the head with symbolic paint or feathers. We then stand before it in an attitude of prayer, holding up the pipe that contains our sacred tobacco, as a gesture that we have freed with honor the spirit of our brother or sister, whose body we were compelled to take to sustain our own life.

When food is taken, the woman murmurs a "grace" — an act so softly and unobtrusively performed that one who does not know the custom usually fails to catch the whisper: "Spirit, partake!"

As her husband receives his bowl or plate, he likewise murmurs his invocation to the spirit. When he becomes an old man, he loves to make a particular effort to prove his gratitude. He cuts off the choicest morsel of the meat and casts it into the fire — the purest and most ethereal element.

Thus we see no need for the setting apart one day in seven as a holy day, since to us all days belong to God.

THE APPRECIATION OF BEAUTY

In the appreciation of beauty, which is closely akin to religious feeling, the American Indian stands alone. In accord with our nature and beliefs, we do not pretend to imitate the inimitable, or to reproduce exactly the work of the Great Artist. That which is beautiful must not be trafficked with, but must only be revered and adored.

I have seen in our midsummer celebrations cool arbors built of fresh-cut branches for council and dance halls, while those who attended decked themselves with leafy boughs, carrying shields and fans of the same, and even making wreaths for their horses' necks. But, strange to say, they seldom make free use of flowers. I once asked the reason for this.

"Why," said one, "the flowers are for our souls to enjoy; not for our bodies to wear. Leave them alone

and they will live out their lives and reproduce themselves as the Great Gardener intended. He planted
them; we must not pluck them, for it would be selfish to
do so."

This is the spirit of the original American. We hold
nature to be the measure of consummate beauty, and
we consider its destruction to be a sacrilege.

I once showed a party of Sioux chiefs the sights of
Washington, and endeavored to impress them with the
wonderful achievements of civilization. After visiting
the Capitol and other famous buildings, we passed
through the Corcoran Art Gallery, where I tried to
explain how the white man valued this or that painting
as a work of genius and a masterpiece of art.

"Ah!" exclaimed an old man, "such is the strange
philosophy of the white man! He hews down the forest
that has stood for centuries in its pride and grandeur,
tears up the bosom of Mother Earth, and causes the
silvery watercourses to waste and vanish away. He ruth-
lessly disfigures God's own pictures and monuments,
and then daubs a flat surface with many colors, and
praises his work as a masterpiece!"

Here we have the root of the failure of the Indian
to approach the "artistic" standard of the civilized
world. It lies not in our lack of creative imagination —
for in this quality we are born artists — it lies rather in
our point of view. Beauty, in our eyes, is always fresh

and living, even as God, the Great Mystery, dresses the world anew at each season of the year.

THE MIRACLE OF THE ORDINARY

We Indians have always been clear thinkers within the scope of our understanding, but cause and effect have not formed the basis for our thinking. We do not chart and measure the vast field of nature or express her wonders in the terms of science; on the contrary, we see miracles on every hand — the miracle of life in seed and egg, the miracle of death in a lightning flash and in the swelling deep!

Nothing of the marvelous can astonish us — a beast could speak or the sun stand still. The virgin birth seems scarcely more miraculous than is the birth of every child that comes into the world, and the miracle of the loaves and fishes excites no greater wonder than the harvest that springs from a single ear of corn.

Let us not forget that even for the most contemporary thinker, who sees a majesty and grandeur in natural law, science cannot explain everything. We all still have to face the ultimate miracle — the origin and principle of life. This is the supreme mystery that is the essence of worship and without which there can be no religion. In the presence of this mystery all peoples must take an attitude much like that of the Indian, who beholds with awe the Divine in all creation.

16

THE WAYS OF THE PEOPLE

*Let those I serve express their thanks according
to their own upbringing and sense of honor.*

— *Ohiyesa*

THE TEACHING OF CHILDREN

I t is commonly supposed that there was no systematic
means of education for Indian children. Nothing could
be further from the truth. All the customs of our people
were held to be divinely instituted, and customs involving
the training of children were scrupulously adhered to and
transmitted from one generation to another.

It is true that we had no schoolhouses, no books, no
regular school hours. Our children were trained in the
natural way — they kept in close contact with the natural world. In this way, they found themselves and
became conscious of their relationship to all of life.

The spiritual world was real to them, and the splendor of life stood out above all else. And beyond all, and in all, was seen to dwell the Great Mystery, unsolved and unsolvable, except in those things that it is good for one's spirit to know.

We taught our children by both example and instruction, but with emphasis on example, because all learning is a dead language to one who gets it second-hand. Our physical training was thorough and intelligent, while as to the moral and spiritual side of our teaching, I am not afraid to compare it with that of any race.

We conceived the art of teaching as, first and foremost, the development of personality; and we considered the fundamentals of education to be love of the Great Mystery, love of nature, and love of people and country.

THE GREAT SONG OF CREATION

Our education begins in our mother's womb. Her attitude and secret meditations are such as to instill into the receptive soul of the unborn child the love of the Great Mystery and a sense of kinship with all creation.

A pregnant Indian woman often chooses one of the great individuals of her family and tribe as a model for her child. This hero is daily called to mind. She gathers from tradition all of his noted deeds and daring exploits, and rehearses them to herself when alone.

In order that the impression might be more distinct, she avoids company. She isolates herself as much as possible, and wanders prayerful in the stillness of the great woods, or on the bosom of the untrodden prairie, not thoughtlessly, but with an eye to the impressions received from the grand and beautiful scenery.

To her poetic mind the imminent birth of her child prefigures the advent of a great spirit — a hero, or the mother of heroes — a thought conceived in the virgin breast of primeval nature, and dreamed out in a hush broken only by the sighing of the pine tree or the thrilling orchestra of a distant waterfall.

And when the day of her days in her life dawns — the day in which there is to be new life, the miracle of whose making has been entrusted to her — she seeks no human aid. She has been trained and prepared in body and mind for this, her holiest duty, ever since she can remember.

She meets the ordeal of childbirth alone, where no curious or pitying eyes might embarrass her; where all nature says to her spirit: "It is love! It is love! The fulfilling of life!"

When, at last, a sacred voice comes to her out of the silence, and a pair of eyes open upon her in the wilderness, she knows with joy that she has borne well her part in the great song of creation!

Presently she returns to the camp, carrying the

mysterious, the holy, the dearest bundle! She feels the endearing warmth of it and hears its soft breathing. It is still a part of herself, since both are nourished by the same mouthful, and no look of a lover could be sweeter than its deep and trusting gaze.

THE CHILD'S FIRST LESSON

The Indian mother has not only the experience of her mother and grandmother, and the accepted rules of her people for a guide, but she humbly seeks to learn a lesson from ants, bees, spiders, beavers, and badgers. She studies the family life of the birds, so exquisite in its emotional intensity and its patient devotion, until she seems to feel the universal mother-heart beating in her own breast.

She continues her spiritual teaching, at first silently — a mere pointing of the index finger to nature — then in whispered songs, bird-like, at morning and evening. To her and to the child the birds are real people, who live very close to the Great Mystery. The murmuring trees breathe its presence; the falling waters chant its praise.

If the child should chance to be fretful, the mother raises her hand. "Hush! Hush!" she cautions it tenderly, "The spirits may be disturbed!" She bids it be still and listen — listen to the silver voice of the aspen, or the clashing cymbals of the birch; and at night she points to the heavenly blazed trail through nature's galaxy of splendor to nature's God. Silence, love, reverence — this is the trinity of the first lessons, and to these she later adds generosity, courage, and chastity.

In due time children take of their own accord the attitude of prayer, and speak reverently of the Powers. They feel that all living creatures are blood brothers and sisters; the storm wind is to them a messenger of the Great Mystery.

THE ROLE OF THE ELDERS

At the age of about eight years, if her child is a boy, the mother turns him over to the father for more disciplined training. If the child is a girl, she is from this time much under the guardianship of her grandmother, who is considered the most dignified protector for the maiden.

The distinctive work of the grandparents is that of acquainting the children with the traditions and beliefs of the nation. The grandparents are old and wise. They have lived and achieved. They are dedicated to the service of the young, as their teachers and advisers, and the young in turn regard them with love and reverence. In them the Indian recognizes the natural and truest teachers of the child.

It is reserved for them to repeat the time-hallowed tales with dignity and authority, so as to lead the child into the inheritance of the stored-up wisdom and experience of the race.

The long winter evenings are considered the proper time for the learning of those traditions that have their roots in the past and lead back to the source of all things. And since the subjects lay half in the shadow of mystery, they have to be taken up at night, the proper realm of mysticism.

Through the telling of these tales, the grandparents inspire love of heroes, pride of ancestry, and devotion to country and people. But these tales do more than enlarge the mind and stimulate the imagination. They furnish the best of memory training, as the child is required to remember and repeat them one by one.

There was usually some old man whose gifts as a storyteller and keeper of wisdom spread his fame far beyond the limits of his immediate family. In his home, at the time of the winter camp, the children of the band were accustomed to gather with more or less regularity.

This was our nearest approach to a school of the woods, and the teacher received his pay not only in gifts of food and other comforts, but chiefly in the love and respect of the village.

A LIFE OF SERVICE

The public position of the Indian has always been entirely dependent upon our private virtue. We are never permitted to forget that we do not live to ourselves alone, but to our tribe and clan. Every child, from the first days of learning, is a public servant in training.

In our traditional ways, the child is kept ever before the public eye, from birth onward. The birth would be announced by the tribal herald, accompanied by a distribution of presents to the old and needy. The same thing would occur when the child took its first step, spoke its first word, had its ears pierced, shot his first game.

Not a step in the child's development was overlooked as an excuse to bring it before the public by giving a feast in its honor. Thus the child's progress was known to the whole clan as to a larger family, and the child grew to adulthood with a sense of reputation to sustain.

At such feasts the parents often gave so generously to the needy that they almost impoverished themselves, thereby setting an example to the child of self-denial for the public good. In this way, children were shown that big-heartedness, generosity, courage, and self-denial are the qualifications of a public servant, and from the cradle we sought to follow this ideal.

The young boy was encouraged to enlist early in the public service, and to develop a wholesome ambition for the honors of a leader and feastmaker, which could never be his unless he proved truthful and generous, as well as brave, and ever mindful of his personal chastity and honor.

As to the young girls, it was the loving parents' pride to have their daughters visit the unfortunate and the helpless, carry them food, comb their hair, and mend their garments. The name "Wenonah," bestowed upon the eldest daughter, means "Bread Giver," or "Charitable One," and a girl who failed in her charitable duties was held to be unworthy of the name.

THE BEAUTY OF GENEROSITY

It has always been our belief that the love of possessions is a weakness to be overcome. Its appeal is to the material part, and if allowed its way it will in time disturb the spiritual balance for which we all strive.

Therefore we must early learn the beauty of generosity. As children we are taught to give what we prize most, that we may taste the happiness of giving; at an early age we are made the family giver of alms. If a child is inclined to be grasping, or to cling too strongly to possessions, legends are related that tell of the contempt and disgrace falling on those who are ungenerous and mean.

Public giving is a part of every important ceremony. It properly belongs to the celebration of birth, marriage, and death, and is observed whenever it is desired to do special honor to any person or event.

Upon such occasions it is common to literally give away all that one has to relatives, to guests of another tribe or clan, but above all to the poor and the aged, from whom we can hope for no return.

Finally, the gift to the Great Mystery, the religious offering, may be of little value in itself, but to the giver's own thought it should carry the meaning and reward of true sacrifice.

ORDER, ETIQUETTE, AND DECORUM

No one who is at all acquainted with us in our homes can deny that we Indians are a polite people.

There are times when we indulge in boisterous mirth — indeed, I have often spent an entire evening at an Indian fireside laughing until I could laugh no more — but the general rule of behavior is gravity and decorum. The enforced intimacy of living in close quarters would soon become intolerable were it not for these instinctive reserves and delicacies; this unfailing respect for the established place and possessions of every other member of the family circle; this habitual quiet, order, and decorum.

Only the aged, who have journeyed far, are in a manner exempt from ordinary rules. Advancing years have earned them freedom, not only from the burden of laborious and dangerous tasks, but from those restrictions of custom and etiquette that are religiously observed by all others.

The old men and women are privileged to say what they please and how they please, without contradiction, while the hardships and bodily infirmities that of necessity fall to their lot are softened so far as may be by universal consideration and attention.

But for the rest of us, a soft, low voice has always been considered an excellent thing, in a man as well as in a woman. Even the warrior who inspired the greatest terror in the hearts of his enemies was, as a rule, a man of the most exemplary gentleness, and almost feminine refinement, among his family and friends. And though we are capable of strong and durable feeling, we are not demonstrative in our affection at any time, especially in the presence of guests or strangers.

It is a rule of the Indian home that the grandfather is master of ceremonies at all times. He is spokesman for the family if a stranger enters. If he is absent, the father or the husband speaks; all others may only smile in greeting. If both men are absent, the grandmother is spokeswoman; if she is away, the mother or wife speaks, with as much dignity as modesty. If no older person is at home, the eldest son or daughter greets the guest, but if they have no brother to speak for them, and an entire stranger enters, the girls may properly observe silence. The stranger should explain the reason for the intrusion.

In the presence of a guest, promiscuous laughing or a careless attitude are not permitted. Rigid decorum and respectful silence are observed, and if any children are present, they must not stare at the stranger. All noisy play and merriment must be kept within familiar family circles, except on the occasion of certain games and dances.

The serving of food is always orderly and polite. Guests are offered food at whatever hour of the day they may appear. The mother of the family serves first the guest, if any, then her father, her husband, her mother, the children in order of age, and, herself last of all. Each person returns the empty dish to her with appropriate words of thanks.

Simple as they seem, these rules and conventions have stood the test of time and are universally respected. In such ways is the natural life of the Indian saved from rudeness and disorder.

THE MORAL STRENGTH OF WOMEN

In the woman is vested the standard of morals of our people. She is the silent but telling power behind all of life's activities.

She rules undisputed in her own domain. The children belong to her clan, not to the clan of the father. She holds all the family property, and the honor of the house is in her hands. All virtue is entrusted to her, and her position is recognized by all.

Possessed of true feminine dignity and modesty, she is expected to be the equal of her mate in physical endurance and skill, and to share equally in the arduous duties of daily life. But she is expected to be superior in spiritual insight.

She is the spiritual teacher of the child, as well as its tender nurse, and she brings its developing soul before the Great Mystery as soon as she is aware of its coming. It is her responsibility to endow her child with nature's gifts and powers, for we believe that from the moment of conception to the end of the second year, it is her spiritual influence that counts for most.

There is nothing artificial about her person, and very little insincerity in her character. Her early and consistent training, the definiteness of her vocation, and, above all, her profoundly religious attitude gives her a strength and poise that cannot be overcome by ordinary misfortune.

It is my belief that no woman of any race has ever come closer to universal motherhood. She is, in fact, the moral salvation of our people.

THE SACREDNESS OF HONOR

A sense of honor pervades all aspects of Indian life.

Orphans and the aged are invariably cared for, not

only by their next of kin, but by the whole clan. The man who is a skillful hunter, and whose wife is alive to her opportunities, makes many feasts, to which he is careful to invite the older men of his clan. He recognizes that they have outlived their period of greatest activity, and now love nothing so well as to eat in good company and live over their past.

He sets no price upon either his property or his labor. His generosity is limited only by his strength. He regards it as an honor to be selected for a difficult or dangerous service, and would think it a shame to ask for any other reward, saying rather: "Let those I serve express their thanks according to their own upbringing and sense of honor."

He is always ready to undertake the impossible, or to impoverish himself for the sake of a friend.

Where the other person is regarded more than the self, duty is sweeter and more inspiring, patriotism more sacred, and friendship is a pure and eternal bond.

THE HONOR OF WARFARE

The common impression that the Indian is naturally cruel and revengeful is entirely opposed to our philosophy and training. Warfare was regarded largely as sort of a game, undertaken in order to develop the manly qualities of our youth.

It was the coming of white traders with their guns,

knives, and whiskey, that roused the revengeful tendencies of the Indian. In our natural state we were neither mean nor deceitful. It is true that men like King Philip, Weatherford, and Little Crow lifted their hands against the white man. But their fathers, Massasoit, Attackullakulla, and Wabasha, had held out their hands with gifts.

In our natural state, it was the degree of risk that brought honor, rather than the number slain, and a brave man would mourn thirty days, with blackened face and loosened hair, for the enemy whose life had been taken.

And while the spoils of war were allowed, this did not extend to appropriation of the other's territory, nor was there any wish to overthrow another nation and enslave its people.

Indeed, if an enemy honored us with a call, his trust was not misplaced, and he went away convinced that he had met with a royal host! Our honor was the guarantee for his safety, so long as he remained within the camp.

It was also a point of honor in the old days to treat a captive with kindness. I remember well an instance that occurred when I was very small.

My uncle brought home two young Ojibwe women who had been captured in a fight between my people and the Ojibwe. Since none of the Sioux war party had been killed, the women received sympathy and were tenderly treated by the Sioux women. They were apparently very happy, although of course they felt deeply the losses sustained at the time of their capture, and they did not fail to show their appreciation of the kindnesses received at our hands.

As I recall now the remarks made by one of them at the time of their final release, they appear to me quite remarkable. They lived in my grandmother's family for two years, and were then returned to their people at a great peace council of the two nations. When they were about to leave, the elder of the two sisters embraced my grandmother, and then spoke somewhat as follows:

"You are a brave woman and a true mother. I understand now why your son bravely conquered our band, and took my sister and myself as captive. I hated him at first, but now I admire him, because he did just what my father, my brother, or my husband would have done had they opportunity. He did even more. He saved us from the tomahawks of his fellow warriors, and brought us to his home to know a noble and a brave woman.

"I shall never forget your many favors shown to us. But I must go. I belong to my tribe and I shall return to them. I will endeavor to be a true woman also, and to teach my boys to be generous warriors like your son."

Her sister chose to remain among the Sioux all her life, and she married one of our young men.

"I shall make the Sioux and the Ojibwe," she said, "to be as brothers."

But it is perhaps Chief Joseph, who conducted that masterly retreat of eleven hundred miles, burdened with his women and children, the old men and the wounded, who best embodied the honor of warfare. Surely he had reason to hate the race who had driven him from his home. Yet it is a fact that while Joseph was in retreat, when he met white visitors and travelers, some of whom were women, he allowed them to pass unharmed, and in at least one instance let them have horses to help them on their way.

RESPECT FOR JUSTICE

Before there were any cities on this continent, before there were bridges to span the Mississippi, before the great network of railroads was even dreamed of, we Indian people had councils which gave their decisions in accordance with the highest ideal of human justice.

Though the occurrence of murder was rare, it was a grave offense, to be atoned for as the council might decree. Often it happened that the slayer was called upon to pay the penalty with his own life.

In such cases, the murderer made no attempt to escape or evade justice. That the crime was committed in the depths of the forest or at dead of night, witnessed by no human eye, made no difference to his mind. He was thoroughly convinced that all is known to the Great Mystery, and hence did not hesitate to give himself up, to stand trial by the old and wise men of the victim's clan.

Even his own family and clan might by no means attempt to excuse or to defend him. But his judges took all the known circumstances into consideration, and if it appeared that he slew in self-defense, or that the provocation was severe, he might be set free after a thirty days' period of mourning in solitude. This ceremonial mourning was a sign of reverence for the departed spirit.

If there were no circumstances justifying the slaying, the murdered man's next of kin were authorized to take the murderer's life. If they refrained from doing so, as often happened, he remained an outcast from the clan.

It is well remembered that Crow Dog, who killed the Sioux chief, Spotted Tail, in 1881 calmly surrendered himself and was tried and convicted by the courts in South Dakota.

The cause of his act was a solemn commission received from his people thirty years earlier. At that time, Spotted Tail had usurped the chieftainship of his people with the aid of the U.S. military. Crow Dog was under a vow to slay the chief, in case he ever disgraced the name of the Brule Sioux.

There is no doubt that Spotted Tail had committed crimes both public and private, having been guilty of misuse of office as well as of gross offense against morality. Therefore, his death was not a matter of personal vengeance, but of just retribution.

A few days before Crow Dog was to be executed, he asked permission to visit his home and say farewell to his wife and twin boys, then nine or ten years old. Strange to say, the request was granted, and the condemned man was sent home under escort of the deputy sheriff, who remained at the Indian agency, merely telling his prisoner to report there on the following day.

When Crow Dog did not appear at the time set, the sheriff dispatched the Indian police after him. They did not find him, and his wife simply said that he had desired to ride alone to the prison, and would reach there on the day appointed. All doubt was removed the next day by a telegram from Rapid City, two hundred miles distant. It said, "Crow Dog has just reported here."

This incident drew public attention, with the unexpected result that the case was reopened, and Crow Dog was acquitted. He returned to his home and lived much respected among his people.

THE DISGRACE OF LYING AND THIEVERY

Such is the importance of our honor and our word that in the early days, lying was a capital offense. Because we believed that the deliberate liar is capable of committing any crime behind the screen of cowardly untruth and double dealing, the destroyer of mutual confidence was summarily put to death, that the evil might go no further.

Likewise, thievery was a disgrace, and if discovered, the name of "wamonon," or Thief, was fixed upon him forever as an unalterable stigma.

The only exception to the rule was in the case of food, which is always free to the hungry if there is none to offer it. Other protection than the moral law there could not be in an Indian community, where there were neither locks nor doors, and everything was open and of easy access to all comers.

FRIENDSHIP

Among our people, friendship is held to be the severest test of character.

It is easy, we think, to be loyal to family and clan, whose blood is in our own veins. Love between man and woman is founded on the mating instinct, and is not free from desire and self-seeking. But to have a friend, and to be true under any and all trials, is the truest mark of a man!

The highest type of friendship is the relation of "brother-friend" or "life-and-death" friend. This bond is between man and man; it is usually formed in early youth, and can only be broken by death.

It is the essence of comradeship and fraternal love, without thought of pleasure or gain, but rather for moral support and inspiration. Each vows to die for the other, if need be, and nothing is denied the brother-friend, but neither is anything required that is not in accord with the highest conception of the Indian mind.

BRAVERY AND COURAGE

As to our personal bravery and courage, no race can outdo us. Even our worst enemies, those who accuse us of treachery, blood-thirstiness, cruelty, and lust, have not denied our courage. But in their minds, our courage is ignorant, brutal, and fanatical. Our own conception of bravery makes of it a high moral virtue, for to us it consists not so much in aggressive self-assertion as in absolute self-control.

The brave man, we contend, yields neither to fear nor anger, desire nor agony. He is at all times master of himself; his courage rises to the heights of chivalry, patriotism, and real heroism.

The Creek war chief, Weatherford, was such a man. After Jackson had defeated the Creeks, he demanded Weatherford, dead or alive. The following night Weatherford presented himself at the general's tent, saying, "I am Weatherford. Do as you please with me. I would still be fighting you had I the warriors to fight with. But they no longer answer my call, for they are dead."

Crazy Horse, too, was a man of true bravery and honor. It was observed that when he pursued the enemy into their stronghold, as he was wont to do, he often refrained from killing, and simply struck them with a switch, showing that he did not fear their weapons nor care to waste his upon them.

"Let neither cold, hunger, nor pain, nor the fear of them, neither the bristling teeth of danger, nor the very jaws of death itself, prevent you from doing a good deed," said an old chief to a scout who was about to seek the buffalo in midwinter for the relief of his starving people. This was our pure and simple conception of courage.

THE REALITY OF PSYCHIC POWERS

It is well accepted that the Indian had well-developed psychic powers.

A Sioux prophet predicted the coming of the white man fully fifty years before the event, and even described accurately his garments and weapons. Before the steamboat was invented, another prophet of our race described the "fire boat" that would swim upon the mighty river, the Mississippi.

Some of us also seem to have a peculiar intuition for the locality of a grave. Those who possess this sensitivity often explain it by saying that they have received a communication from the spirit of the departed.

My own grandmother was one of these. As far back as I can remember, when camping in a strange country, my brother and I would search for and find human bones at the spot she had indicated to us as an ancient burial-place or the spot where a lone warrior had fallen. Of course, the outward signs of burial had long since been obliterated.

She had other remarkable premonitions or intuitions that I recall. I heard her speak of a peculiar sense in the breast, by which, as she said, she was advised of anything of importance concerning her absent children. Other native women have claimed a similar monitor, but I never heard of one who could interpret it with such accuracy.

We were once camping on Lake Manitoba when we received news that my uncle and his family had been murdered several weeks before at a fort some two hundred miles distant. While all our clan were wailing and mourning, my grandmother calmly bade them cease, saying that her son was approaching, and that they would see him shortly.

Although we had no other reason to doubt the ill

tidings, it is a fact that my uncle came into camp two days after his reported death.

At another time, when I was fourteen years old, we had just left Fort Ellis on the Assiniboine River, and my youngest uncle had selected a fine spot for our night camp. It was already after sundown, but my grandmother became unaccountably nervous, and positively refused to pitch her tent.

So we reluctantly went on down the river, and camped after dark at a secluded place. The next day we learned that a family who were following close behind had stopped at the place first selected by my uncle, but were surprised in the night by a roving war-party, and all were massacred. This incident made a great impression on our people.

Many of us believe that one may be born more than once, and there are some who claim to have full knowledge of a former incarnation. There are also those who believe in a "twin spirit" born into another tribe or race.

There once was a well-known Sioux war-prophet who lived in the middle of the last century, so that he is still remembered by the old men of his band. After he had reached middle age, he declared that he had a spirit brother among the Ojibwe, the ancestral enemies of the Sioux. He even named the band to which his brother belonged, and said that he also was a war-prophet among his people.

Upon one of their hunts along the border between the two tribes, the Sioux leader one evening called his warriors together, and solemnly declared to them that they were about to meet a like band of Ojibwe hunters, led by his spirit twin.

Since this was to be their first meeting since they were born as strangers, he earnestly begged the young men to resist the temptation to join battle with their tribal foes.

"You will know him at once," the prophet said to them, "for he will not only look like me in face and form, but he will display the same totem, and even sing my war songs!"

They sent out scouts, who soon returned with news of the approaching party. Then the leading men started with their peace pipe for the Ojibwe camp, and when they were near at hand they fired three distinct volleys, a signal of their desire for a peaceful meeting. The response came in like manner, and they entered the camp with the peace pipe in the hands of the prophet.

Lo, the stranger prophet advanced to meet them, and the people were greatly struck with the resemblance between the two men, who met and embraced each other with unusual fervor.

It was quickly agreed by both parties that they

should camp together for several days, and one evening the Sioux made a "warriors' feast" to which they invited many of the Ojibwe. The prophet asked his twin brother to sing one of his sacred songs, and behold, it was the very song that he himself was wont to sing.

No doubt many such stories were altered and shaded after the fact, and unquestionably, false prophets and conjurers abounded during the times of tribulation when the white races overtook our people. But I know that our people possessed remarkable powers of concentration and abstraction, and I believe that such nearness to nature as I have described keeps the spirit sensitive to impressions not commonly felt, and in touch with the unseen powers.

THE MEANING OF DEATH

Our attitude toward death, the test and background of life, is entirely consistent with our character and philosophy. Certainly we never doubt the immortal nature of the human soul or spirit, but neither do we care to speculate upon its probable state or condition in a future life.

The idea of a "happy hunting ground" is modern, and probably borrowed from or invented by the white man. In our original belief we were content to believe that the spirit which the Great Mystery breathed into us returns to the Creator who gave it, and that after it is freed from the body it is everywhere and pervades all nature.

Thus, death holds no terrors for us. We meet it with simplicity and perfect calm, seeking only an honorable end as our last gift to our family and descendants. Therefore we court death in battle but consider it disgraceful to be killed in a private quarrel. If we are dying at home, it is customary to have our bed be carried out of doors as the end approaches, so that our spirit may pass under the open sky.

Next to this, the matter that concerns us most is the parting with our dear ones, especially if we have any little children who must be left behind to suffer want. Our family affections are strong, so those of us left behind grieve intensely for those who pass, even though we have unbounded faith in a spiritual companionship and believe that the spirit of the departed lingers near the grave or "spirit bundle" for the consolation of friends, and is able to hear prayers.

Our outward signs of mourning for the dead are far more spontaneous and convincing than the correct and well-ordered black-clothed manners of civilization. Both men and women among us loosen our hair and cut it according to the degree of relationship and devotion.

Consistent with the ideal of sacrificing all personal beauty and adornment, we trim off likewise from the dress its fringes and ornaments, perhaps cut it short, or cut the robe or blanket in two.

Men blacken their faces, and widows or bereaved parents sometimes gash their arms and legs until they are covered with blood. Giving themselves up wholly to their grief, they are no longer concerned about any earthly possession, and often give away all that they have, even their beds and their home, to the first comers.

The wailing for the dead continues night and day to the point of utter voicelessness; it is a musical, weird, and heart-piercing sound, which has been compared to the "keening" of the Celtic mourner.

I recall a touching custom among us, which was designed to keep the memory of the departed near and warm in the bereaved household. A lock of hair of the beloved dead was wrapped in pretty clothing, something it was supposed that he or she would like to wear if living. This "spirit bundle," as it was called, was suspended from a tripod, and occupied a place of honor in the lodge. At every meal time, a dish of food was placed under it, and some person of the same sex and age as the one who once was must afterward be invited in to partake of the food. At the end of a year from the time of death, the relatives made a public feast and gave away the clothing and other gifts, while the lock of hair was interred with appropriate ceremonies.

Even the slaying of an enemy required proper

respect for the dead. Though it was considered no sin to take the life of a man in battle, still, the slayer of the man was expected to mourn for thirty days, blackening his face and loosening his hair according to the custom. This ceremonial mourning was a sign of reverence for the departed spirit.

So much reverence was due the departed spirit that it was not customary with us even to name the dead aloud.

17

THE COMING OF
THE WHITE WAYS

Long before I heard of Christ or saw a white man . . . I knew God. I perceived what goodness is. I saw and loved what is really beautiful. Civilization has not taught me anything better!

— *Ohiyesa*

THE EFFECT OF THE WHITE RELIGION

Our transition from our natural life to the artificial life of civilization has resulted in great spiritual and moral loss.

In effect, the European who came among us said, "You are a child. You cannot make or invent anything. We have the only God, and He has given us authority to teach and govern all the peoples of the earth. In proof of this we have His Book, a supernatural guide, every word of which is true and binding. We are a chosen people — a superior race. We have a heaven with golden gates fenced in from all pagans and unbelievers,

and a hell where the souls of such are tortured eternally. We are honorable, truthful, refined, religious, peaceful; we hate cruelty and injustice; our business is to educate, Christianize, and protect the rights and property of the weak and the uncivilized."

Those of us who listened to the preaching of the missionaries came to believe that the white man alone had a real God, and that the things which the Indian had previously held sacred were inventions of the devil. This undermined the very foundations of our philosophy. It very often did so without substituting the Christian philosophy, not because the innate qualities of the Christian philosophy were unworthy, but because the inconsistent behavior of its advocates made it hard for us to accept or understand.

A few of us did, in good faith, accept the white man's God. The black-robed preacher was like the Indian himself in seeking no soft things, and as he followed the fortunes of the tribes in the wilderness, the tribesmen learned to trust and to love him.

Then came other missionaries who had houses to sleep in, and gardens planted, and who hesitated to sleep in the Indian's wigwam or eat of his wild meat, but for the most part held themselves aloof and urged their own dress and ways upon their converts. These, too, had their following in due time.

But in the main it is true that while the Indian eagerly sought guns and gunpowder, knives and whiskey, a few articles of dress, and, later, horses, he did not of himself desire the white man's food, his houses, his books, his government, or his religion.

The two great "civilizers," after all, were whiskey and gunpowder, and from the hour we accepted these we had in reality sold our birthright, and all unconsciously consented to our own ruin.

Once we had departed from the broad democracy and pure idealism of our prime, and had undertaken to enter upon the world's game of competition, our rudder was unshipped, our compass lost, and the whirlwind and tempest of materialism and love of conquest tossed us to and fro like leaves in a wind.

THE HYPOCRISY OF THE CHRISTIANS AMONG US

There was undoubtedly much in primitive Christianity to appeal to the Indians, and Jesus' hard sayings to the rich and about the rich were entirely comprehensible to us. Yet the religion that we heard preached in churches and saw practiced by congregations, with its element of display and self-aggrandizement, its active proselytism, and its open contempt of all religions but its own, was for a long time extremely repellent.

I am reminded of a time when a missionary undertook to instruct a group of our people in the truth of his holy religion. He told them of the creation of the earth in six days, and of the fall of our first parents by eating an apple.

My people were courteous, and listened attentively; and after thanking the missionary, one man related in his own turn a very ancient tradition concerning the origin of the maize. But the missionary plainly showed his disgust and disbelief, indignantly saying, "What I delivered to you were sacred truths, but this that you tell me is mere fable and falsehood!"

"My brother," gravely replied the offended Indian, "it seems that you have not been well grounded in the rules of civility. You saw that we, who practice these rules, believed your stories. Why, then, do you refuse to credit ours?"

Who may condemn our belief? Surely not the devout Catholic, or even the Protestant missionary who teaches Bible miracles as literal fact! The logical person must either deny all miracles or none, and our American Indian myths and hero stories are no less credible than those of the Hebrews of old.

Strange as it may seem, it is true that in our secret soul we despised the good men who came to convert and enlighten us! To our mind, the professionalism of the pulpit, the paid exhorter, the moneyed church, was an unspiritual and unedifying thing, and it was not until our spirit was broken and our moral and physical constitution undermined by trade, conquest, and strong drink, that the Christian missionaries obtained any real hold upon us.

Nor were its proselytism and hypocrisy the only elements in the alien religion that offended us. We found it shocking and almost incredible that among this race that claimed to be superior there were many who did not even pretend to profess the faith. Not only did they not profess it, but they stooped so low as to insult their God with profane and sacrilegious speech! In our own tongue the name of God was not spoken aloud, even with utmost reverence, much less lightly and irreverently.

More than this, even in those white men who professed religion we found much inconsistency of conduct. They spoke much of spiritual things, while seeking only the material. They bought and sold everything: time, labor, personal independence, the love of woman, and even the ministrations of their holy faith!

The higher and spiritual life, though first in theory, was clearly secondary, if not entirely neglected, in practice.

THE TRUE SPIRIT OF JESUS

This lust for money, power, and conquest did not escape moral condemnation at our hands, nor did we fail to contrast this conspicuous trait of the dominant race with the spirit of the meek and lowly Jesus.

I remember the words of one old battle-scarred warrior. I was at the time meeting with groups of young men — Sioux, Cheyenne, Cree, Ojibwe, and others — in log cabins or little frame chapels trying to set before them in simple language the life and character of the man Jesus.

The old warrior got up and said, "Why, we have followed this law you speak of for untold ages! We owned nothing, because everything is from the Creator. Food was free, land as free as sunshine and rain. Who has changed all this? The white man. And yet he says he is a believer in God! He does not seem to inherit any of the traits of his Father, nor does he follow the example set by his brother Christ."

Another of the older men, called upon for his views, kept a long silence. Finally, he said, "I have come to the conclusion that this Jesus was an Indian. He was opposed to material acquisition and to great possessions. He was inclined to peace. He was as unpractical as any Indian and set no price upon his labor of love. These are not the principles upon which the white man has founded his civilization. It is strange that he could not rise to these simple principles which were so commonly observed among our people."

CHRISTIAN CIVILIZATION

In time we came to recognize that the drunkards and licentious among white men, with whom we too frequently came in contact, were condemned by the white man's religion as well, and must not be held to discredit it. But it was not so easy to overlook or to excuse national bad faith. When distinguished emissaries from the

Father at Washington, some of them ministers of the Gospel and even bishops, came to the Indian nations, and pledged to us in solemn treaty the national honor, with prayer and mention of their God; and when such treaties, so made, were promptly and shamelessly broken, is it strange that the action should arouse not only anger, but contempt?

The historians of the white race admit that the Indian was never the first to repudiate his oath.

I confess I have wondered much that Christianity is not practiced by the very people who vouch for that wonderful conception of exemplary living. It appears that they are anxious to pass on their religion to all other races, but keep very little of it for themselves. I have not yet seen the meek inherit the earth, or the peacemakers receive high honor.

It is my personal belief, after thirty five years' experience of it, that there is no such thing as "Christian civilization." I believe that Christianity and modern civilization are opposed and irreconcilable, and that the spirit of Christianity and of our ancient religion is essentially the same.

LAMENT FOR A LOST VISION

Long before I ever heard of Christ or saw a white man, I had learned the essence of morality.

With the help of dear Nature herself, my grandmother taught me things simple but of mighty import.

I knew God. I perceived what goodness is. I saw and loved what is really beautiful. Civilization has not taught me anything better!

As a child, I understood how to give. I have forgotten that grace since I became civilized. I lived the natural life, whereas I now live the artificial.

Any pretty pebble was valuable to me then; every growing tree an object of reverence. Now I worship with the white man before a painted landscape whose value is estimated in dollars!

In this manner is the Indian rebuilt, as the natural rocks are ground to powder, and made into artificial blocks which may be built into the walls of modern society.

THE GIFT OF MY PEOPLE

I am an Indian; and while I have learned much from civilization, I have never lost my Indian sense of right and justice.

When I reduce civilization to its most basic terms, it becomes a system of life based on trade. Each man stakes his powers, the product of his labor, his social, political, and religious standing against his neighbor. To gain what? To gain control over his fellow workers, and the results of their labor.

Is there not something worthy of perpetuation in our Indian spirit of democracy, where Earth, our mother, was free to all, and no one sought to impoverish or enslave his neighbor? Where the good things of Earth were not ours to hold against our brothers and sisters, but were ours to use and enjoy together with them, and with whom it was our privilege to share?

Indeed, our contribution to our nation and the world is not to be measured in the material realm. Our greatest contribution has been spiritual and philosophical. Silently, by example only, in wordless patience, we have held stoutly to our native vision of personal faithfulness to duty and devotion to a trust. We have not advertised our faithfulness nor made capital of our honor.

But again and again we have proved our worth as citizens of this country by our constancy in the face of hardship and death. Prejudice and racial injustice have been no excuse for our breaking our word. This simplicity and fairness has cost us dear. It has cost us our land and our freedom, and even the extinction of our race as a separate and unique people.

But, as an ideal, we live and will live, not only in the splendor of our past, the poetry of our legends and art, not only in the interfusion of our blood with yours, and in our faithful adherence to the ideals of American citizenship, but in the living heart of the nation.

The spirit of the Native people, the first people, has never died. It lives in the rocks and the forests, the rivers and the mountains. It murmurs in the brooks and whispers in the trees. The hearts of these people were formed of the earth that we now walk, and their voice can never be silenced.

— *Kent Nerburn*

PART 3

THE WISDOM OF THE GREAT CHIEFS

The Classic Speeches of Chief Red Jacket, Chief Joseph, and Chief Seattle

18

CHIEF RED JACKET

"We do not wish to destroy your religion, or to take it from you. We only want to enjoy our own."

— *Chief Red Jacket, 1805*

INTRODUCTION

The Seneca people were part of the great Iroquois federation of tribes that lived in the area we now know as upstate New York. This federation of tribes, also known as the Five Nations (or the Six Nations after the addition of the Tuscarora), was unique among Native peoples in the sophistication of its political organization. The Six Nations lived in a rough geographic line extending from the eastern edge of New York to the western. They called this territory their "long house," and each tribe had its place and its role.

The Senecas were the westernmost tribe, and were responsible for what was known as the "western door" of the long house. When a visitor or messenger came

to this western door, it was the responsibility of the Senecas to assay the purpose of the visit. If it was something of little consequence, they were empowered to dispose of it in their own council. But if the subject under consideration proved to be something of importance to all the tribes of the federation, a runner was sent to call for a general meeting. The tribes then gathered and discussed the issue at hand, listening and speaking until common understanding had been reached.

It was this practice of government by council and consensus that fostered the oratorical genius of the people of the Iroquois federation. The need to discuss ideas clearly and directly, and to arrive at decisions which all could support, bred in the Iroquois an eloquence that European observers often compared to that of the Roman Senate.

It was to this tradition that Red Jacket was heir, and he undertook the task of oratorical training with extreme diligence. He studied other great speakers and their subtleties of style. He worked on musicality and nuance, and he strove to master the use of metaphor and poetic expression.

By the time he had achieved prominence in his tribe, he was capable of oratorical expression so full of nuance and poetry that government agent Horatio Jones called his oratorical talents "among the noblest that nature ever conferred upon man."

The speech quoted here was given in the summer of 1805. Its occasion was a meeting of the assembled chiefs of the Iroquois federation. They had gathered in council to hear the request of a young missionary named Cram, who had been sent among them by the Evangelical Missionary Society of Massachusetts. This society had sent missionaries before, and had met with some success. But the Indians apparently had not taken as fully to Christianity as the society had hoped. The society now hoped to establish Cram among the Iroquois so as to further their education in the Christian religion.

Cram spoke briefly, requesting only the right to follow up on the interest that certain of the Indians had shown in the Christian religion. After hearing him, the chiefs consulted for about two hours. Then Red Jacket rose and spoke.

F riend and brother, it was the will of the Great Spirit that we should meet together this day. He orders all things, and He has given us a fine day for our council. He has taken his garment from before the sun and has caused it to shine with brightness upon us.

Our eyes are opened so that we see clearly. Our ears are unstopped so that we have been able to distinctly hear the words which you have spoken.

For all these favors we thank the Great Spirit and Him only.

Brother, this council fire was kindled by you. It was at your request that we came together at this time. We have listened with attention to what you have said.

You have requested us to speak our minds freely. This gives us great joy, for we now consider that we stand upright before you, and can speak what we think. All have heard your voice and all speak to you now as one man. Our minds are agreed.

Brother, you say that you want an answer to your talk before you leave this place. It is right that you should have one, as you are a great distance from home, and we do not wish to detain you. But we will first look back a little, and tell you what our fathers have told us, and what we have heard from the white people.

Brother, listen to what we say.

There was a time when our forefathers owned this great island. [The Seneca, like many other tribes, refer to this continent as a "great island."] Their seats extended from the rising to the setting of the sun. The Great Spirit had made it for the use of Indians. He had created the buffalo, the deer, and other animals for food. He had made the bear and the beaver, and their skins served us for clothing. He had scattered them over the country, and had taught us how to take them. He had caused the earth to produce corn for bread.

All this He had done for His red children because He loved them.

If we had any disputes about hunting grounds, they were generally settled without the shedding of much blood. But an evil day came upon us. Your forefathers crossed the great waters and landed upon this island.

Their numbers were small. They found friends and not enemies. They told us they had fled from their own country for fear of wicked men, and had come here to enjoy their religion.

They asked for a small seat. We took pity on them, granted their request, and they sat down amongst us.

We gave them corn and meat. They gave us poison [rum] in return.

The white people, brother, had now found our country. Tidings were carried back and more came amongst us. Yet we did not fear them. We took them to be friends.

They called us brothers. We believed them and gave them a larger seat.

At length their numbers had greatly increased.

They wanted more land. They wanted our country.

Our eyes were opened, and our minds became uneasy.

Wars took place. Indians were hired to fight against Indians, and many of our people were destroyed.

They also brought strong liquor among us. It was strong and powerful and has slain thousands.

Brother, our seats were once large, and yours were very small. You have now become a great people, and we have scarcely a place left to spread our blankets. You have got our country, but you are not satisfied. You want to force your religion upon us.

Brother, continue to listen.

You say that you are sent to instruct us how to worship the Great Spirit agreeably to His mind, and if we do not take hold of the religion which you white people teach we shall be unhappy hereafter.

You say that you are right, and we are lost.

How do we know this to be true?

We understand that your religion is written in a book. If it was intended for us as well, why has not the Great Spirit given it to us; and not only to us, but why did He not give to our forefathers the knowledge of that book, with the means of understanding it rightly? We know only what you tell us about it. How shall we know when to believe, being so often deceived by the white people?

Brother, you say there is but one way to worship

and serve the Great Spirit. If there is but one religion, why do you white people differ so much about it? Why not all agree, as you can all read the book?

Brother, we do not understand these things.

We are told that your religion was given to your forefathers and has been handed down, father to son. We also have a religion which was given to our forefathers, and has been handed down to us, their children.

We worship in that way. It teaches us to be thankful for all the favors we receive, to love each other, and to be united. We never quarrel about religion.

Brother, the Great Spirit has made us all. But He has made a great difference between His white and red children. He has given us a different complexion and different customs. To you He has given the arts; to these He has not opened our eyes. We know these things to be true.

Since He has made so great a difference between us in other things, why may we not conclude that He has given us a different religion, according to our understanding?

The Great Spirit does right. He knows what is best for His children. We are satisfied.

Brother, we do not wish to destroy your religion, or to take it from you. We only want to enjoy our own.

Brother, you say you have not come to get our land or our money, but to enlighten our minds. I will now tell you that I have been at your meetings and saw you collecting money from the meeting.

I cannot tell you what the money was intended for, but suppose it was for your minister; and if we should conform to your way of thinking, perhaps you should want some from us.*

Brother, we are told that you have been preaching to the white people in this place. These people are our neighbors. We are acquainted with them. We will wait a little while, and see what effect your preaching has upon them. If we find it does them good and makes them honest and less disposed to cheat Indians, we will then consider again what you have said.

Brother, you have now heard our answer to your talk, and this is all we have to say at present. As we are going to part, we will come and take you by the hand, and hope the Great Spirit will protect you on your journey, and return you safe to your friends.

At the end of the speech, Red Jacket rose and approached the missionary with his hand extended. The missionary refused to take it.

---

* This paragraph doesn't appear in the first recorded edition of the speech, recorded by James D. Bemis in 1811. It does appear in later transcriptions by other authors. Its particularity and pointedness do not seem in keeping with the speech's general tone, but I have chosen to include it, despite reservations about its authenticity.

19

CHIEF JOSEPH

*"The earth is the mother of all people, and all
people should have equal rights upon it."*
— *Chief Joseph, 1879*

INTRODUCTION

Chief Joseph of the Nez Perce is considered by
Native and non-Native people alike as one of the
greatest of all Indian leaders. "Buffalo Bill" Cody
called Joseph "the greatest Indian America ever produced." Edward Curtis, who devoted much of his life
to photographing the American Indian, said of Joseph,
"I think he was one of the greatest men who ever
lived."

Such words were not without justification. Joseph
was a singular man with a deep and abiding sense of
justice and an unshakable love for his people and the
land to which they were born. He was unfailingly fair

in his dealings with everyone he met, and unceasing in his efforts to serve the good of his people.

Joseph assumed the chieftaincy of the Nez Perce people upon the death of his father in 1871. He inherited a situation of almost impossible complexity. In 1854 the Nez Perce bands had unwillingly signed a treaty with the United States in an effort to protect their homelands. There is some question as to whether Joseph's father actually signed this treaty, but it is clear that he was radically opposed to the idea.

While this treaty had significantly reduced the size of the Nez Perce lands, it had also guaranteed their sovereignty over the land that remained. But gold had been discovered in 1860, and almost overnight entire settlements had appeared on Nez Perce land in direct violation of this treaty.

The United States had then pressured the Nez Perce to sign another treaty cutting the size of their land even further. The Nez Perce had disagreed over the wisdom of signing this new treaty, which would have diminished their lands by another 90 percent, and had dissolved their federation. Joseph's father had been among those refusing to sign. Another chief had then made the treaty with the U.S., and in this treaty had signed over the lands of Joseph's band.

Shortly afterward, Joseph assumed the chieftaincy of his band, and settlers began pouring into his land based on the conditions of the treaty his father had never signed.

Joseph, who was a supremely honorable man, found himself in the middle of a deeply troubling situation. He would not give up his homeland, which his father had sworn him to preserve, but he did not wish to do harm to the struggling white settlers who had come to his valley innocently and in good faith.

In an effort to keep his land for his people, Joseph called a council and instructed the settlers to leave. Eventually a presidential decree supported his position, but within a year the Commissioner of Indian Affairs reversed this decree without informing Joseph.

The series of events that followed eventually led Joseph to take his people, along with the other non-treaty Indians, on the famous thousand-mile flight through the rugged country of Oregon, Idaho, and Montana, in an attempt to get to Canada where they could live in peace.

The Nez Perce had never looked upon their exodus as a fight. Indeed, they fought only when necessary to facilitate their flight and to protect their elderly and children. Joseph endeavored to keep the tempers of his warriors under control, and he even helped white settlers he encountered along the way.

But the flight became a major media event throughout the United States. The government was not about to allow a group of Indian refugees traveling with elderly, women, and infants to escape from the massed forces of the U.S. military.

On October 5, 1877, only forty miles from the freedom of Canada, the Nez Perce were faced with a heart-rending decision. The military had once again surrounded them. The warriors determined that they could elude capture, but to do so would require them to leave their elderly, wounded, and children behind. This they would not do.

And so it was, after discussing the matter with the other Nez Perce chief, that Joseph rode forth under the early winter sky of the Bear Paw foothills and spoke his now-famous words to the representatives of the U.S. military: "From where the sun now stands, I will fight no more forever."

He did not do this as a surrender. He felt confident that reinforcements from Sitting Bull were on the way, and that he could prevail if he waited. But he had been promised by the U.S. general that if both sides laid down their arms, the Nez Perce could return to their home. In Joseph's mind, it had been the offer of an armistice, and he had accepted it because the 184 women and 147 children with him were freezing and starving.

But the government soon failed to keep the promise of its general. Joseph and his Nez Perce were moved to North Dakota, and then to Kansas, where an epidemic of malaria ravaged what remained of his people

It was against this backdrop that Joseph came to Washington to plead the cause of his people. On January 14, 1879, barely a year after he had submitted his people to the U.S. military on that raw and blustery October day, Joseph stood in Lincoln Hall in Washington, D.C., before an assembly of congressmen, diplomats, and dignitaries, and delivered the following speech.

We cannot know the exact words he spoke that evening; the version that has come down to us was published several months later in a distinguished periodical, *The North American Review*. But we can surmise, from the version we do have, that in those two hours he painted one of the most poignant portraits of the Indian experience that has ever been voiced by any American.

The speech is often quoted, but seldom reproduced in its entirety due to its length. But that length is deceptive. Joseph speaks in simple, straightforward sentences that lead us relentlessly through the events that reduced his people from a peaceful, prosperous nation to a disease-ridden remnant living in squalor, without food or medicine, on inhospitable lands.

His logic is unassailable; his contained passion,

riveting. He speaks with candor and clarity, sparing no one in the unflinching honesty of his narrative. It is a speech of pathos and power, anger and dignity. Perhaps more than any other, this speech embodies the experience of the Native American after the arrival of the European on North American soil.

My friends, I have been asked to show you my heart. I am glad to have a chance to do so. I want the white people to understand my people.

Some of you think an Indian is like a wild animal. This is a great mistake. I will tell you all about our people, and then you can judge whether an Indian is a man or not.

I believe much trouble would be saved if we opened our hearts more. I will tell you in my way how the Indian sees things. The white man has more words to tell you how they look to him, but it does not require many words to speak the truth.

What I have to say will come straight from my heart, and I will speak with a straight tongue. The Great Spirit is looking at me, and will hear me.

My name is In-mut-too-yah-lat-lat [Thunder Traveling over Mountains]. I am chief of the Wal-lam-wat-kin band of the Chute-pa-lu, or Nez Perce. I was born in eastern Oregon, thirty-eight winters ago.

My father was chief before me. When a young man, he was called Joseph by Mr. Spaulding, a missionary. He died a few years ago. He left a good name on earth. He advised me well for my people.

Our fathers gave us many laws, which they had learned from their fathers. These laws were good. They told us to treat all men as they treated us, that we should never be the first to break a bargain, that it was a disgrace to tell a lie, that we should speak only the truth, that it was a shame for one man to take from another his wife or his property without paying for it.

We were taught to believe that the Great Spirit sees and hears everything, and that He never forgets; that hereafter He will give every man a spirit-home according to his deserts: If he has been a good man, he will have a good home; if he has been a bad man, he will have a bad home.

This I believe, and all my people believe the same.

We did not know there were other people besides the Indian until about one hundred winters ago, when some men with white faces came to our country. They brought many things with them to trade for furs and skins. They brought tobacco, which was new to us. They brought guns with flint stones on them, which frightened our women and children. Our people could not talk with these white-faced men, but they used signs which all people understand.

These men were called Frenchmen, and they called our people "Nez Perce," because they wore rings in their noses for ornaments. Although very few of our people wear them now, we are still called by the same name.

These French trappers said a great many things to our fathers, which have been planted in our hearts. Some were good for us, but some were bad.

Our people were divided in opinion about these

men. Some thought they taught more bad than good. An Indian respects a brave man, but he despises a coward. He loves a straight tongue, but he hates a forked tongue. The French trappers told us some truths and some lies.

The first white men of your people who came to our country were named Lewis and Clark. They also brought many things that our people had never seen. They talked straight, and our people gave them a great feast as a proof that their hearts were friendly.

These men were very kind. They made presents to our chiefs and our people made presents to them. We had a great many horses, of which we gave them what they needed, and they gave us guns and tobacco in return.

All the Nez Perce made friends with Lewis and Clark, and agreed to let them pass through their country, and never to make war on white men. This promise the Nez Perce have never broken. No white man can accuse them of bad faith and speak with a straight tongue. It has always been the pride of the Nez Perce that they were the friends of the white men.

When my father was a young man there came to our country a white man [Rev. Henry H. Spaulding] who talked spirit law. He won the affections of our people because he spoke good things to them. At first he did not say anything about white men wanting to settle on our lands. Nothing was said about that until about twenty winters ago, when a number of white people came into our country and built houses and made farms.

At first our people made no complaint. They thought there was room enough for all to live in peace, and they were learning many things from the white men that seemed to be good.

But we soon found that the white men were growing rich very fast, and were greedy to possess everything the Indian had. My father was the first to see through the schemes of the white men, and he warned his tribe to be careful about trading with them. He had suspicion of men who seemed anxious to make money.

I was a boy then, but I remember well my father's caution. He had sharper eyes than the rest of our people.

Next there came a white officer [Governor Isaac Stevens of the Washington Territory], who invited all the Nez Perce to a treaty council. After the council was opened he made known his heart. He said there were a great many white people in our country, and many more would come; that he wanted the land marked out so that the Indians and the white men could be separated. If they were to live in peace it was necessary, he said, that the Indians should have a country set apart for them, and in that country they must stay.

My father, who represented his band, refused to

have anything to do with the council, because he wished to be a free man. He claimed that no man owned any part of the earth, and a man could not sell what he did not own.

Mr. Spaulding took hold of my father's arm and said, "Come and sign the treaty."

My father pushed him away, and said, "Why do you ask me to sign away my country? It is your business to talk to us about spirit matters and not to talk to us about parting with our land."

Governor Stevens urged my father to sign his treaty, but he refused. "I will not sign your paper," he said. "You go where you please, so do I. You are not a child. I am no child. I can think for myself. No man can think for me. I have no home other than this. I will not give it up to any man. My people would have no home. Take away your paper. I will not touch it with my hand."

My father left the council. Some of the chiefs of the other bands of the Nez Perce signed the treaty, and then Governor Stevens gave them presents of blankets. My father cautioned his people to take no presents, for "after a while," he said, "they will claim that you have accepted pay for your country."

Since that time four bands of the Nez Perce have received annuities from the United States. My father was invited to many councils, and they tried hard to make him sign the treaty, but he was firm as the rock, and would not sign away his home. His refusal caused a difference among the Nez Perce.

Eight years later [1863] was the next treaty council. A chief called Lawyer, because he was a great talker, took the lead in the council, and sold nearly all the Nez Perce country.

My father was not there. He said to me: "When you go into council with the white man, always remember your country. Do not give it away. The white man will cheat you out of your home. I have taken no pay from the United States. I have never sold our land."

In this treaty Lawyer acted without authority from our band. He had no right to sell the Wallowa country. The Wallowa country, which means "the land of winding water," is in the northeastern part of what is now the state of Oregon. It is the ancestral home of Joseph's band of the Nez Perce.] That had always belonged to my father's own people, and the other bands had never disputed our right to it. No other Indians ever claimed Wallowa.

In order to have all people understand how much land we owned, my father planted poles around it and said, "Inside is the home of my people. The white man may take the land outside. Inside this boundary all our people were born. It circles around the graves of our fathers, and we will never give up these graves to any man."

The United States claimed they had bought all the Nez Perce country outside the Lapwai Reservation from Lawyer and other chiefs. But we continued to live on this land in peace until eight years ago, when white men began to come inside the boundaries my father had set.

We warned them against this great wrong, but they would not leave our land, and some bad blood was raised. The white men represented that we were going upon the warpath. They reported many things that were false.

The United States government again asked for a treaty council. My father had become blind and feeble. He could no longer speak for his people. It was then that I took my father's place as chief. In this council I made my first speech to white men.

I said to the agent who held the council: "I did not want to come to this council, but I came hoping that we could save blood. The white man has no right to come here and take our country. We have never accepted any presents from the government. Neither Lawyer nor any other chief had authority to sell this land. It has always belonged to my people. It came unclouded to them from our fathers, and we will defend this land as long as a drop of Indian blood warms the hearts of our men."

The agent said he had orders from the Great White Chief at Washington for us to go upon the Lapwai Reservation, and that if we obeyed, he would help us in many ways.

"You must move to the agency," he said.

I answered him, "I will not. I do not need your help. We have plenty, and we are contented and happy if the white man will let us alone. The reservation is too small for so many people with all their stock. You can keep your presents. We can go to your towns and pay for all we need. We have plenty of horses and cattle to sell, and we won't have any help from you. We are free now; we can go where we please. Our fathers were born here. Here they lived, here they died, here are their graves. We will never leave them."

The agent went away and we had peace for a little while.

Soon after this my father sent for me. I saw he was dying. I took his hand in mine. He said, "My son, my body is returning to my mother earth, and my spirit is going very soon to see the Great Spirit Chief. When I am gone, think of your country. You are the chief of these people. They look to you to guide them. Always remember that your father never sold this country. You must stop your ears whenever you are asked to sign a treaty selling your home. A few years more, and white men will be all around you. They have their eyes on this land. My son, never forget my dying words. This country holds your father's body. Never sell the bones of your father and mother."

I pressed my father's hand and told him I would protect his grave with my life. My father smiled and passed away to the spirit land.

I buried him in that beautiful valley of winding waters. I love that land more than all the rest of the world. A man who would not love his father's grave is worse than a wild animal.

For a short time we lived quietly. But this could not last. White men had found gold in the mountains around the land of winding water. They stole many horses from us, and we could not get them back because we were Indians.

The white men told lies for each other. They drove off a great many of our cattle. Some white men branded our young cattle so they could claim them.

We had no friend who would plead our cause before the law councils. It seemed to me that some of the white men in Wallowa were doing these things on purpose to get up a war. They knew that we were not strong enough to fight them.

I labored hard to avoid trouble and bloodshed. We gave up some of our country to the white men, thinking that then we could have peace.

We were mistaken. The white man would not let us

alone.

We could have avenged our wrongs many times, but we did not. Whenever the government has asked us to help them against other Indians, we have never refused. When the white men were few and we were strong, we could have killed them all off, but the Nez Perce wished to live at peace.

If we have not done so, we have not been to blame. I believe that the old treaty has never been correctly reported. If we ever owned the land we own it still, for we never sold it.

In the treaty councils the commissioners have claimed that our country had been sold to the government. Suppose a white man should come to me and say, "Joseph, I like your horses, and I want to buy them."

I say to him, "No, my horses suit me. I will not sell them."

Then he goes to my neighbor and says to him, "Joseph has some good horses. I want to buy them, but he refuses to sell."

My neighbor answers, "Pay me the money, and I will sell you Joseph's horses."

The white man returns to me and says, "Joseph, I have bought your horses, and you must let me have them."

If we sold our lands to the government, this is the way they were bought.

On account of the treaty made by the other bands of the Nez Perce, the white men claimed my lands. We were troubled greatly by white men crowding over the line. Some of these were good men, and we lived on peaceful terms with them. But they were not all good.

Nearly every year the agent came over from Lapwai and ordered us on to the reservation. We always replied that we were satisfied to live in Wallowa. We were careful to refuse presents or annuities which he offered.

Through all the years since the white men came to Wallowa, we have been threatened and taunted by them and the treaty Nez Perce. They have given us no rest.

We have had a few good friends among white men, and they have always advised my people to bear these taunts without fighting. Our young men were quick-tempered, and I have had great trouble in keeping them from doing rash things.

I have carried a heavy load on my back ever since I was a boy. I learned then that we were but few, while the white men were many, and that we could not hold our own with them.

We were like deer. They were like grizzly bears.

We had a small country. Their country was large.

We were contented to let things remain as the Great Spirit Chief made them. They were not, and would change the rivers and the mountains if they did not suit them.

Year after year we have been threatened, but no war was made upon my people until General Howard came to our country two years ago and told us he was the white war-chief of all that country. He said, "I have a great many soldiers at my back. I am going to bring them up here, and then I will talk to you again. I will not let white men laugh at me the next time I come. The country belongs to the government, and I intend to make you go upon the reservation."

I remonstrated with him against bringing more soldiers to the Nez Perce country. He had one house full of troops all the time at Fort Lapwai.

The next spring the agent at Umatilla agency sent an Indian runner to tell me to meet General Howard at Walla Walla. I could not go myself, but I sent my brother and five other head men to meet him, and they had a long talk.

General Howard said, "You have talked straight, and it is all right. You can stay in Wallowa."

He insisted that my brother should go with him to Fort Lapwai. When the party arrived there General Howard sent out runners and called all the Indians in to a grand council. I was in that council.

I said to General Howard, "We are ready to listen."

He answered that he would not talk then, but would hold a council next day, when he would talk plainly.

I said to General Howard, "I am ready to talk today. I have been in a great many councils, but I am no wiser. We are all sprung from a woman, although we are unlike in many things. We cannot be made over again. You are as you were made, and as you were made you can remain. We are just as we were made by the Great Spirit, and you cannot change us. Then why should children of one mother and one father quarrel? Why should one try to cheat the other? I do not believe that the Great Spirit Chief gave one kind of men the right to tell another kind of men what they must do."

General Howard replied, "You deny my authority, do you? You want to dictate to me, do you?"

Then one of my chiefs — Too-hool-hool-suit — rose in the council and said to General Howard, "The Great Spirit Chief made the world as it is, and as He wanted it, and He made a part of it for us to live upon. I do not see where you get authority to say that we shall not live where He placed us."

General Howard lost his temper and said, "Shut up! I don't want to hear any more of such talk. The law says you shall go upon the reservation to live, and I want you to do so. But you persist in disobeying the law. If you do not move, I will take the matter into my own hand and make you suffer for your disobedience."

Too-hool-hool-suit answered, "Who are you, that

you should ask us to talk, and then tell me I shan't talk? Are you the Great Spirit? Did you make the world? Did you make the sun? Did you make the rivers to run for us to drink? Did you make the grass to grow? Did you make all these things, that you talk to us as though we were boys? If you did, then you have the right to talk as you do."

General Howard replied, "You are an impudent fellow, and I will put you in the guard house," and then ordered a soldier to arrest him.

Too-hool-hool-suit made no resistance. He asked General Howard, "Is that your order? I don't care. I have expressed my heart to you. I have nothing to take back. I have spoken for my country. You can arrest me, but you cannot change me or make me take back what I have said."

The soldiers came forward and seized my friend and took him to the guard house. My men whispered among themselves whether they should let this thing be done.

I counseled them to submit. I knew if we resisted that all the white men present, including General Howard, would be killed in a moment, and we would be blamed. If I had said nothing, General Howard would never have given another unjust order against my men.

I saw the danger, and while they dragged Too-hool-hool-suit to prison, I arose and said, "I am going to talk now. I don't care whether you arrest me or not."

I turned to my people and said, "The arrest of Too-hool-hool-suit was wrong, but we will not resent the insult. We were invited to this council to express our hearts, and we have done so." Too-hool-hool-suit was prisoner for five days before he was released.

The council broke up for that day. On the next morning General Howard came to my lodge and invited me to go with him and White Bird and Looking Glass to look for land for my people.

As we rode along we came to some good land that was already occupied by Indians and white people. General Howard, pointing to this land, said, "If you will come on to the reservation, I will give you these lands and move these people off."

I replied, "No. It would be wrong to disturb these people. I have no right to take their homes. I have never taken what did not belong to me. I will not now."

We rode all day upon the reservation, and found no good land unoccupied. I have been informed by men who do not lie that General Howard sent a letter that night telling the soldiers at Walla Walla to go to Wallowa valley and drive us out upon our return home.

In the council, next day, General Howard informed me, in a haughty spirit, that he would give my people thirty days to go back home, collect all their stock, and move onto the reservation, saying, "If you are not here in that time, I shall consider that you want to fight, and will send my soldiers to drive you on."

I said, "War can be avoided, and it ought to be avoided. I want no war. My people have always been the friends of the white man. Why are you in such a hurry? I cannot get ready to move in thirty days. Our stock is scattered, and the Snake River is very high. Let us wait until fall. Then the river will be low. We want time to hunt up our stock and gather supplies for winter."

General Howard replied, "If you let the time run over one day, the soldiers will be there to drive you onto the reservation, and all your cattle and horses outside of the reservation at that time will fall into the hands of the white men."

I knew I had never sold my country, and that I had no land in Lapwai. But I did not want bloodshed. I did not want my people killed. I did not want anybody killed.

Some of my people had been murdered by white men, and the white murderers were never punished for it. I told General Howard about this, and again said I wanted no war. I wanted the people who lived upon the lands I was to occupy at Lapwai to have time to gather their harvest.

I said in my heart that, rather than have war, I would give up my country. I would give up my father's grave. I would give up everything rather than have the blood of white men upon the hands of my people.

General Howard refused to allow me more than thirty days to move my people and their stock. I am sure that he began to prepare for war at once.

When I returned to Wallowa I found my people very much excited upon discovering that the soldiers were already in the Wallowa valley. We held a council and decided to move immediately, to avoid bloodshed.

Too-hool-hool-suit, who felt outraged by his imprisonment, talked for war, and made many of my young men willing to fight rather than be driven like dogs from the land where they were born. He declared that blood alone would wash out the disgrace General Howard had put upon him. It required a strong heart to stand up against such talk, but I urged my people to be quiet, and not to begin a war.

We gathered all the stock we could find, and made an attempt to move. We left many of our horses and cattle in Wallowa, and we lost several hundred in crossing the river. All of my people succeeded in getting across in safety.

Many of the Nez Perce came together in Rocky Canyon to hold a grand council. I went with all my people. This council lasted ten days. There was a great deal of war talk, and a great deal of excitement. There was one young brave present whose father had been killed by a white man five years before. This man's blood was bad against white men, and he left the council calling for revenge.

Again I counseled peace, and I thought the danger was past.

We had not complied with General Howard's order because we could not, but we intended to do so as soon as possible. I was leaving the council to kill beef for my family when news came that the young man whose father had been killed had gone out with several other hot-blooded young braves and killed four white men.

He rode up to the council and shouted, "Why do you sit here like women? The war has begun already."

I was deeply grieved. All the lodges were moved except my brother's and my own. I saw clearly that the war was upon us when I learned that my young men had been secretly buying ammunition. I heard then that Too-hool-hool-suit, who had been imprisoned by General Howard, had succeeded in organizing a war party.

I knew that their acts would involve all my people. I saw that the war could not be prevented. The time had passed.

I counseled peace from the beginning. I knew that we were too weak to fight the United States. We had many grievances, but I knew that war would bring more.

We had good white friends, who advised us against taking the war path. My friend and brother, Mr. Chapman, who has been with us since the surrender, told us just how the war would end. Mr. Chapman took sides against us, and helped General Howard. I do not blame him for doing so. He tried hard to prevent bloodshed.

We hoped the white settlers would not join the soldiers. Before the war commenced we had discussed this matter all over, and many of my people were in favor of warning them that if they took no part against us they should not be molested in the event of war being begun by General Howard.

This plan was voted down in the war council.

There were bad men among my people who had quarreled with white men, and they talked of their wrongs until they roused all the bad hearts in the council. Still, I could not believe they would begin the war.

I know that my young men did a great wrong, but I ask, "Who was first to blame?" They had been insulted a thousand times. Their fathers and brothers had been killed. Their mothers and wives had been disgraced. They had been driven to madness by whiskey sold to them by white men. They had been told by General Howard that all their horses and cattle which they had been unable to drive out of Wallowa were to fall into the hands of white men. And, added to all this, they were homeless and desperate.

I would have given my own life if I could have undone the killing of white men by my people.

I blame my young men and I blame the white men. I blame General Howard for not giving my people time to get their stock away from Wallowa. I do not acknowledge that he had the right to order me to leave Wallowa at any time. I deny that either my father or myself ever sold that land. It is still our land. It may never again be our home, but my father sleeps there, and I love it as I love my mother. I left there hoping to avoid bloodshed.

If General Howard had given me plenty of time to gather up my stock, and treated Too-hool-hool-suit as a man should be treated, there would have been no war.

My friends among white men have blamed me for the war. I am not to blame. When my young men began the killing, my heart was hurt. Although I did not justify them, I remembered all the insults I had endured, and my blood was on fire. Still, I would have taken my people to the buffalo country without fighting if possible. I could see no other way to avoid a war.

We moved over to White Bird Creek, sixteen miles away, and there encamped, intending to collect our stock before leaving. But the soldiers attacked us, and the first battle was fought.

We numbered in that battle sixty men, and the soldiers a hundred. The fight lasted but a few minutes, when the soldiers retreated before us for twelve miles. They lost thirty-three killed, and had seven wounded.

When an Indian fights, he only shoots to kill. But soldiers shoot at random. None of the soldiers were scalped. We do not believe in scalping, nor in killing wounded men. Soldiers do not kill many Indians unless they are wounded and left upon the battle field. Then they kill Indians.

Seven days after the first battle, General Howard arrived in the Nez Perce country, bringing seven hundred more soldiers. It was now war in earnest.

We crossed the Salmon River, hoping General Howard would follow. We were not disappointed. He did follow us, and we got back between him and his supplies, and cut him off for three days.

He sent out two companies to open the way. We attacked them, killing one officer, two guides, and ten men.

We withdrew, hoping the soldiers would follow. But they had got enough fighting for that day. They entrenched themselves, and next day we attacked them again. The battle lasted all day, and was renewed next morning. We killed four and wounded seven or eight.

About this time General Howard found out that we were in his rear. Five days later he attacked us with three hundred and fifty soldiers and settlers. We had two hundred and fifty warriors.

The fight lasted twenty-seven hours. We lost four killed and several wounded. General Howard's loss was twenty-nine men killed and sixty wounded.

The following day the soldiers charged upon us, and we retreated with our families and stock a few miles, leaving eighty lodges to fall into General Howard's hands.

Finding that we were outnumbered, we retreated to the Bitterroot valley. Here another body of soldiers came upon us and demanded our surrender.

We refused.

They said, "You cannot get by us."

We answered, "We are going by you without fighting if you will let us. But we are going by you anyhow."

We then made a treaty with these soldiers. We agreed not to molest anyone, and they agreed that we might pass through the Bitterroot country in peace.

We bought provisions and traded stock with the white men there.

We understood that there was to be no more war. We intended to go peaceably to the buffalo country, and leave the question of returning to our country to be settled afterward.

With this understanding, we traveled on for four days. And, thinking that the trouble was all over, we stopped and prepared tent poles to take with us.

We started again, and at the end of two days saw three white men passing our camp. Thinking that peace had been made, we did not molest them. We could have killed them or taken them prisoners, but we did not suspect them of being spies, which they were.

That night the soldiers surrounded our camp. About daybreak one of my men went out to look after his horses. The soldiers saw him and shot him down like a coyote.

I have since learned that these soldiers were not those we had left behind. They had come upon us from another direction.

The new white war chief's name was Gibbon. He charged upon us while some of my people were still asleep. We had a hard fight. Some of my men crept around and attacked the soldiers from the rear. In this battle we lost nearly all our lodges, but we finally drove General Gibbon back.

Finding that he was not able to capture us, he sent to his camp a few miles away for his big guns [cannons]. But my men had captured them and all the ammunition.

We damaged the big guns all we could, and carried away the powder and the lead.

In the fight with General Gibbon we lost fifty women and children and thirty fighting men. We remained long enough to bury our dead. The Nez

Perce never make war on women and children. We could have killed a great many women and children while the war lasted, but we would feel ashamed to do so cowardly an act.

We never scalp our enemies. But when General Howard came up and joined General Gibbon, their Indian scouts dug up our dead and scalped them. I have been told that General Howard did not order this great shame to be done.

We retreated as rapidly as we could toward the buffalo country. After six days General Howard came close to us, and we went out and attacked him, and captured nearly all his horses and mules. We then marched on to the Yellowstone Basin.

On the way we captured one white man and two white women. We released them at the end of three days. They were treated kindly. The women were not insulted. Can the white soldiers tell me of one time when Indian women were taken prisoners and held three days, and then released without being insulted? Were the Nez Perce women who fell into the hands of General Howard's soldiers treated with as much respect? I deny that a Nez Perce was ever guilty of such a crime.

A few days later we captured two more white men. One of them stole a horse and escaped. We gave the other a poor horse and told him he was free.

Nine days' march brought us to the mouth of Clark's Fork of the Yellowstone. We did not know what had become of General Howard, but we supposed that he had sent for more horses and mules.

He did not come up, but another new war chief [General Sturgis] attacked us. We held him in check while we moved all our women and children and stock out of danger, leaving a few men to cover our retreat.

Several days passed, and we heard nothing of General Howard, or Gibbon, or Sturgis. We had repulsed each in turn, and began to feel secure, when another army, under General Miles, struck us. This was the fourth army, each of which outnumbered our fighting force, that we had encountered within sixty days.

We had no knowledge of General Miles's army until a short time before he made a charge upon us, cutting our camp in two and capturing nearly all of our horses.

About seventy men, myself among them, were cut off. My little daughter, twelve years old, was with me. I gave her a rope and told her to catch a horse and join the others who were cut off from the camp. I have not seen her since, but I have learned that she is alive and well.

I thought of my wife and children, who were now surrounded by soldiers, and I resolved to go to them or die.

With a prayer in my mouth to the Great Spirit Chief who rules above, I dashed unarmed through the line of soldiers. It seemed to me that there were guns on every side, before and behind me.

My clothes were cut to pieces and my horse was wounded, but I was unharmed. As I reached the door of my lodge, my wife handed me my rifle, saying, "Here's your gun. Fight!"

The soldiers kept up a continuous fire.

Six of my men were killed in one spot near me. Ten or twelve soldiers charged into our camp and got possession of two lodges, killing three Nez Perce and losing three of their men, who fell inside our lines.

I called my men to drive them back.

We fought at close range, not more than twenty steps apart, and drove the soldiers back upon their main line, leaving their dead in our hands.

We secured their arms and ammunition. We lost, the first day and night, eighteen men and three women. General Miles lost twenty-six killed and forty wounded.

The following day General Miles sent a messenger into my camp under protection of a white flag. I sent my friend Yellow Bull to meet him.

Yellow Bull understood the messenger to say that General Miles wished me to consider the situation, that he did not want to kill my people unnecessarily. Yellow Bull understood this to be a demand for me to surrender and save blood.

Upon reporting this message to me, Yellow Bull said he wondered whether General Miles was in earnest. I sent him back with my answer, that I had made up my mind, but would think about it and send word soon.

A little later he sent some Cheyenne scouts with another message. I went out to meet them.

They said they believed that General Miles was sincere and really wanted peace.

I walked to General Miles's tent. He met me and we shook hands. He said, "Come, let us sit down by the fire and talk this matter over."

I remained with him all night. Next morning Yellow Bull came over to see if I was alive, and why I did not return.

General Miles would not let me leave the tent to see my friend alone.

Yellow Bull said to me, "They have got you in their power, and I am afraid they will never let you go again. I have an officer in our camp, and I will hold him until they let you go free."

I said, "I do not know what they mean to do with me, but if they kill me you must not kill the officer. It will do no good to avenge my death by killing him."

Yellow Bull returned to my camp.

I did not make any agreement that day with

General Miles. The battle was renewed while I was with him. I was very anxious about my people. I knew that we were near Sitting Bull's camp in King George's land, and I thought maybe the Nez Perce who had escaped would return with assistance. No great damage was done to either party during the night.

On the following morning I returned to my camp by agreement, meeting the officer who had been held a prisoner in my camp at the flag of truce.

My people were divided about surrendering. We could have escaped from Bear Paw Mountain if we had left our wounded, old men, and children behind. We were unwilling to do this. We had never heard of a wounded Indian recovering while in the hands of white men.

On the evening of the fourth day, General Howard came in with a small escort, together with my friend Chapman. We could now talk understandingly.

General Miles said to me in plain words, "If you will come out and give up your arms, I will spare your lives and send you to your reservation." I do not know what passed between General Miles and General Howard.

I could not bear to see my wounded men and women suffer any longer. We had lost enough already.

General Miles had promised that we might return to our own country with what stock we had left. I thought we could start again. I believed General Miles, or I never would have surrendered.

I have heard that he has been censured for making the promise to return us to Lapwai. He could not have made any other terms with me at that time. I would have held him in check until my friends came to my assistance, and then neither of the generals nor their soldiers would have ever left Bear Paw Mountain alive.

On the fifth day I went to General Miles and gave up my gun, and said, "From where the sun now stands I will fight no more."

My people needed rest. We wanted peace.

I was told we could go with General Miles to Tongue River and stay there until spring, when we would be sent back to our country.

Finally it was decided that we were about to be taken to Tongue River. We had nothing to say about it. After our arrival at Tongue River, General Miles received orders to take us to Bismarck. The reason given was that subsistence would be cheaper there.

General Miles opposed this order. He said, "You must not blame me. I have endeavored to keep my word, but the chief who is over me has given the order, and I must obey it or resign. That would do you no good. Some other officer would carry out the order."

I believe General Miles would have kept his word if he could have done so. I do not blame him for what we have suffered since the surrender. I do not know who is to blame. We gave up all our horses — over eleven hundred — and all our saddles — over one hundred — and we have not heard from them since. Someone has got our horses.

General Miles turned my people over to another soldier, and we were taken to Bismarck.

Captain Johnson, who now had charge of us, received an order to take us to Leavenworth. At Leavenworth we were placed on a low river bottom, with no water except river water to drink and cook with.

We had always lived in a healthy country, where the mountains were high and the water was cold and clear. Many of my people sickened and died, and we buried them in this strange land.

I cannot tell how much my heart suffered for my people while at Leavenworth. The Great Spirit Chief who rules above seemed to be looking some other way, and did not see what was being done to my people.

During the hot days we received notice that we were to be moved farther away from our own country. We were not asked if we were willing to go.

We were ordered to get into railroad cars. Three of my people died on the way to Baxter Springs [Kansas]. It was worse to die there than to die fighting in the mountains.

We were moved from Baxter Springs to the Indian Territory, and set down without our lodges. We had but little medicine, and we were nearly all sick.

Seventy of my people have died since we moved there.

We have had a great many visitors who have talked many ways.

Some of the chiefs from Washington came to see us, and selected land for us to live upon. We have not moved to that land, for it is not a good place to live.

The Commissioner Chief [E. A. Hayt] came to see us. I told him, as I told everyone, that I expected General Miles's word would be carried out.

He said it could not be done; that white men now lived in my country and all the land was taken up; that if I returned to Wallowa, I could not live in peace; that law-papers were out against my young men who began the war; and that the government could not protect my people.

This talk fell like a heavy stone upon my heart.

I saw that I could not gain anything by talking to him. Other law chiefs came to see me and said they would help me get a healthy country.

I did not know who to believe. The white men have too many chiefs. They do not understand each other. They do not all talk alike.

The Commissioner Chief invited me to go with

him and hunt for a better home than we have now. I like the land we found [west of the Osage Reservation] better than any place I have seen in that country.

But it is not a healthy land. There are no mountains and rivers. The water is warm. It is not a good country for stock.

I do not believe my people can live there. I am afraid they will all die. The Indians who occupy that country are all dying off. I promised Chief Hayt to go there and do the best I could until the government got ready to make good General Miles's word. I was not satisfied, but I could not help myself.

Then the Inspector Chief [General McNeill] came to my camp and we had a long talk. He said I ought to have a home in the mountain country north, and that he would write a letter to the Great Chief at Washington. Again the hope of seeing the mountains of Idaho and Oregon grew up in my heart.

At last I was granted permission to come to Washington and bring my friend Yellow Bull and our interpreter with me. I am glad we came. I have shaken hands with a great many friends.

But there are some things I want to know which no one seems able to explain.

I cannot understand how the government sends a man out to fight us, as it did General Miles, and then breaks his word. Such a government has something wrong about it.

I cannot understand why so many chiefs are allowed to talk so many different ways, and promise so many different things. I have seen the Great Father Chief [president], the next Great Chief [secretary of the Interior], the Commissioner Chief [Hayt], the Law Chief [General Butler], and many other law chiefs [congressmen], and they all say they are my friends, and that I shall have justice. But while their mouths all talk right I do not understand why nothing has been done for my people.

I have heard talk and talk, but nothing is done. Good words do not last long unless they amount to something.

Words do not pay for my dead people. They do not pay for my country, now overrun by white men. They do not protect my father's grave. They do not pay for all my horses and cattle.

Good words will not give me back my children. Good words will not make good the promise of your War Chief General Miles. Good words will not give my people good health and stop them from dying. Good words will not get my people a home where they can live in peace and take care of themselves.

I am tired of talk that comes to nothing.

It makes my heart sick when I remember all the good words and the broken promises.

There has been too much talking by men who had no right to talk. Too many misrepresentations have been made; too many misunderstandings have come up between the white men about the Indians.

If the white man wants to live in peace with the Indian he can live in peace. There need be no trouble. Treat all men alike. Give them the same law. Give them all an even chance to live and grow.

All men were made by the same Great Spirit Chief. They are all brothers. The earth is the mother of all people, and all people should have equal rights upon it.

You might as well expect the rivers to run backward as that any man who was born a free man should be contented when penned up and denied liberty to go where he pleases. If you tie a horse to a stake, do you expect he will grow fat? If you pen an Indian up on a small spot of earth and compel him to stay there, he will not be contented, nor will he grow and prosper.

I have asked some of the great white chiefs where they get their authority to say to the Indian that he shall stay in one place, while he sees white men going where they please. They cannot tell me.

I only ask of the government to be treated as all other men are treated. If I cannot go to my own home, let me have a home in some country where my people will not die so fast.

I would like to go to the Bitterroot valley. There my

people would be healthy; where they are now, they are dying. Three have died since I left my camp to come to Washington.

When I think of our condition my heart is heavy. I see men of my race treated as outlaws and driven from country to country, or shot down like animals.

I know that my race must change. We cannot hold our own with the white men as we are. We only ask an even chance to live as other men live.

We ask to be recognized as men. We ask that the same law shall work alike on all men. If the Indian breaks the law, punish him by the law. If the white man breaks the law, punish him also.

Let me be a free man — free to travel, free to stop, free to work, free to trade where I choose, free to choose my own teachers, free to follow the religion of my fathers, free to think and talk and act for myself — and I will obey every law, or submit to the penalty.

When the white man treats an Indian as they treat each other, then we will have no more wars. We shall all be alike — brothers of one father and one mother, with one sky above us and one government for all.

Then the Great Spirit Chief who rules above will smile upon this land, and send rain to wash out the bloody spots made by brothers' hands from the face of the earth.

For this time the Indian race are waiting and praying.

I hope that no more groans of wounded men and women will ever go to the ear of the Great Spirit Chief above, and that all people may be one people.

In-mut-too-yah-lat-lat has spoken for his people.

Joseph died in 1904, twenty-five years after delivering this speech. He was still confined on a reservation far from his ancestral homeland.

Dr. E. H. Latham, the agency physician who had attended Joseph for the last fourteen years of his life, explained the cause of death simply: "Chief Joseph died of a broken heart. . . ."

20

CHIEF SEATTLE

"We may be brothers after all. We shall see."
— *Chief Seattle, 1853*

INTRODUCTION

No speech ever given by an Indian leader has been so widely quoted, or so widely revered, as the speech given by Chief Seattle of the Suquamish people in 1853.

Its setting was a cold December day on the shores of the area the Indians called "the Whulge," and the white people called Puget Sound in what is now the state of Washington. Over a thousand Indians had gathered to await the arrival of a ship carrying Isaac Stevens, who had recently been appointed by President Pierce to serve as the governor of the newly created Washington Territory. The Indians knew little about

Stevens, but they knew that he carried their fate in his hands. Their vigil on the wintry shores was as much an act of curiosity as a gesture of respect.

When the ship carrying Stevens arrived, the new governor stepped on shore without ceremony. He was a diminutive man, brusque in his manner and direct in his approach to people and problems. He had been appointed to facilitate the settling of the area, and to do so he had to remove the native inhabitants so they would not impede the progress of the white settlers. He was anxious to get on with the matter.

He began speaking in rapid-fire sentences that even the interpreters were hard pressed to understand. Little was clear to the Indian people, except that this man intended to remove them from their ancestral lands and place them on prison plots of earth he called "reservations."

When Stevens was done speaking, the Indians turned toward Chief Seattle. He had long been recognized as the leader of the allied tribes of the Whulge. It was only natural that he should speak for them all.

Seattle was a thoughtful man. Though he had achieved his early reputation by his military prowess, it had always been his conviction that talk toward peace was preferable to actions toward war. When the whites had begun arriving in the 1830s, he had welcomed them, and even converted to their Christian religion.

While other tribes had banded together to resist this foreign encroachment, Seattle had kept his people of the Whulge as far from battle as he could.

Even after 1851, when the emigration across the Oregon Trail had brought legions of settlers into the Northwest, Seattle had continued to believe that the bounty of the land would provide for all, and he had continued to help the settlers establish a life on his beloved Whulge.

But as the years had progressed, and white settlement had increased, Seattle had come to realize that the two cultures could not easily coexist. Indian willingness to share the land had been interpreted by the settlers as an offer of permanent ownership. The Indian tradition of gift-giving was being exploited by the more commerce-minded whites who were intent upon advantage, not fairness and honor. Even the white justice system was encroaching on the Indian ways: Disagreements between Indians were being adjudicated by the white government, even though the Indians had given them no authority to do so.

Seattle knew that the haughty little man who had emerged from the ship represented the end of the Indians' dreams and visions as a free people.

So it was with a sense of sadness, mixed with no little contempt and scorn, that Seattle, the friend and benefactor of the white immigrants, rose to speak in response to the new governor.

He chose his words carefully, and, as was the Indian way, he spoke clearly and from the heart. When he had finished, he had uttered one of the most moving eulogies, and prescient admonitions, ever spoken by any man or woman in any language.

His words have been preserved in many documents. Some of these used a later text which was actually a playwright's literary reworking of the speech. The version we reproduce here is the version transcribed by Dr. Henry Smith as he sat on the shores of the Whulge, listening to Seattle speak.

It is as close to the original version as we are likely to get.

Yonder sky that has wept tears of compassion upon my people for centuries untold, and which to us appears changeless and eternal, may change. Today is fair. Tomorrow it may be overcast with clouds.

My words are like the stars that never change. Whatever Seattle says, the Great Chief at Washington can rely upon with as much certainty as he can upon the return of the sun or the seasons.

The White Chief [Governor Stevens] says that the Big Chief at Washington sends us greetings of friendship and goodwill. This is kind of him, for we know he has little need of our friendship in return.

His people are many. They are like the grass that covers vast prairies.

My people are few. They resemble the scattered trees of a storm-swept plain.

The Great Chief sends us word that he wishes to buy our lands, but is willing to allow us enough to live comfortably. This indeed appears just, even generous, for the red man no longer has rights that he need respect. And the offer may be wise also, as we are no longer in need of an extensive country.

There was a time when our people covered the land as the waves of a wind-ruffled sea cover its shell-paved floor. But that time long since passed away with the greatness of tribes that are now but a mournful memory.

I will not dwell upon, nor mourn over, our untimely decay, nor reproach my white brothers with hastening it, as we too may have been somewhat to blame.

Youth is impulsive. When our young men grow angry at some real or imaginary wrong, and disfigure their faces with black paint, it denotes that their hearts are black, and that they are often cruel and relentless, and our old men and old women are unable to restrain them.

Thus it has ever been. Thus it was when the white man first began to push our forefathers westward.

But let us hope that the hostilities between us may never return. We have everything to lose and nothing to gain.

Revenge by young men is considered gain, even at the cost of their own lives. But old men who stay at home in times of war, and mothers who have sons to lose, know better.

Our good father at Washington — for I presume he is now our father as well as yours, since King George has moved his boundaries further north — our great and good father, I say, sends us word that if we do as he desires, he will protect us. His brave warriors will be to us a bristling wall of strength, and his wonderful ships of war will fill our harbor so that our ancient enemies far to the northward — the Haidas and the Tshimshian — will cease to frighten our women, children, and old men.

Then in reality will he be our father and we his

children.

But can that ever be?

Your God is not our God. Your God loves your people and hates mine. He folds His strong protecting arms lovingly about the white man and leads him by the hand as a father leads his infant son. But He has forsaken His red children — if they are really His.

Our God, the Great Spirit, seems also to have forsaken us. Your God makes your people wax strong every day. Soon they will fill all the land. Our people are ebbing away like a rapidly receding tide that will never return.

The white man's God cannot love our people or He would protect them. They seem to be orphans who can look nowhere for help.

How then can we be brothers? How can your God become our God and renew our prosperity and awaken in us dreams of returning greatness?

If we have a common heavenly father He must be partial — or He came to his white children. We never saw Him. He gave you laws but had no word for His red children whose teeming multitudes once filled this vast continent as stars fill the firmament.

No, we are two distinct races with separate origins and separate destinies. There is little in common between us.

To us, the ashes of our ancestors are sacred, and

their resting place is hallowed ground. You wander far from the graves of your ancestors, and seemingly without regret.

Your religion was written upon tablets of stone by the iron finger of your God so that you could not forget. The red man could never comprehend nor remember it.

Our religion is the traditions of our ancestors — the dreams of our old men, given them in the solemn hours of night by the Great Spirit, and the visions of our sachems — and is written in the hearts of our people.

Your dead cease to love you and the land of their nativity as soon as they pass the portals of the tomb and wander way beyond the stars. They are soon forgotten and never return.

Our dead never forget the beautiful world that gave them being. They still love its verdant valleys, its murmuring rivers, its magnificent mountains, sequestered vales and verdant-lined lakes and bays, and ever yearn in tender, fond affection over the lonely hearted living, and often return from the Great Beyond to visit, guide, console, and comfort them.

Day and night cannot dwell together. The red man has ever fled the approach of the white man, as the morning mist flees before the morning sun.

However, your proposition seems fair and I think that my people will accept it and will retire to the reservation you offer them. Then we will dwell in peace, for the words of the Great White Chief seem to be the words of nature speaking to my people out of dense darkness.

It matters little where we pass the remnant of our days. They will not be many. The Indians' night promises to be dark. Not a single star of hope hovers above his horizon.

Sad-voiced winds moan in the distance. Grim fate seems to be on the red man's trail, and wherever he goes he will hear the approaching footsteps of his fell destroyer and prepare stolidly to meet his doom, as does the wounded doe that hears the approaching footsteps of the hunter.

A few more moons, a few more winters — and not one of the descendants of the mighty hosts that once moved over this broad land or lived in happy homes, protected by the Great Spirit, will remain to mourn over the graves of a people once more powerful and hopeful than yours.

But why should I mourn at the untimely fate of my people? Tribe follows tribe, and nation follows nation, like the waves of the sea. It is the order of nature, and regret is useless.

Your time of decay may be distant, but it surely will come. For even the white man, whose God talked with him as friend with friend, cannot be exempt from the common destiny.

We may be brothers after all. We shall see.

We will ponder your proposition and when we decide, we will let you know. But should we accept it, I here and now make this condition, that we will not be denied the privilege without molestation of visiting at any time the tombs of our ancestors, friends, and children.

Every part of this soil is sacred in the estimation of my people. Every hillside, every valley, every plain and grove, has been hallowed by some sad or happy event in days long vanished.

Even the rocks, which seem to be dumb and dead as they swelter in the sun along the silent shore, thrill with memories of stirring events connected with the lives of my people. And the very dust upon which you now stand responds more lovingly to their footsteps than to yours, because it is rich with the blood of our ancestors and our bare feet are conscious of the sympathetic touch.

Our departed braves, fond mothers, glad, happy-hearted maidens, and even our little children who lived here and rejoiced here for a brief season, will love these somber solitudes, and at eventide they greet shadowy returning spirits.

And when the last red man shall have perished, and the memory of my tribe shall have become a myth among the white men, these shores will swarm with the invisible dead of my tribe.

And when your children's children think themselves alone in the field, the store, the shop, upon the highway, or in the silence of the pathless woods, they will not be alone.

In all the earth there is no place dedicated to solitude. At night, when the streets of your cities and villages are silent, and you think them deserted, they will throng with the returning hosts that once filled them and still love this beautiful land. The white man will never be alone.

Let him be just and deal kindly with my people. For the dead are not powerless.

Dead, did I say? There is no death. Only a change of worlds.

BIOGRAPHICAL NOTES

Aseenewub
Red Lake Ojibwe (19th century)
Also known as Little Rock. He was part of the 1863 treaty negotiations where the U.S. government surrounded the Ojibwe negotiators with cannon and threatened them with hanging if they did not sign over their land.

Big Elk
Omaha Chief (ca. 1772–1842)
A great peacemaker, although he led war parties on the Pawnees. Also a renowned orator. Once painted by

George Catlin. Traveled to Washington, D.C., to sign peace treaties.

Black Elk
Oglala Sioux (ca. 1863–1950)

Medicine man and spiritual leader. Witnessed the Battle of Big Horn at the age of thirteen. Once fled to Canada with his family to avoid being sent to a reservation. Had many dreams and mystical experiences. Dictated his life story in the well-known book, *Black Elk Speaks: The Life Story of a Holy Man of the Oglala Sioux.*

Black Hawk
Sauk and Fox Brave (1767–1838)

Black Hawk's mission in life was to right the wrong he saw done in 1804, when William Henry Harrison plied four chiefs of Black Hawk's tribe with drink so they would sign away the Sauk's land. He encouraged the British to make war with the Americans to stop their westward movement. When even the little land his people had saved began to be squatted on by settlers, Black Hawk went to battle. He eventually became a prisoner of war for several months, then was sent home a folk hero of sorts, hailed by non-Indians as a symbol of the old wild west. In a last insult his dead body was desecrated by vandals.

Canassatego

Onondaga (date and birth unknown–1750)

Canassatego represented the Iroquois in negotiations with the British. Probably killed by pro-French Iroquois.

Charles Alexander Eastman (Ohiyesa)

Santee Sioux (1858–1939)

An author and the first Native American physician. He was born in Redwood Falls, Minnesota. Received a B.S. degree from Dartmouth and attended medical school at Boston University. Was instrumental in founding the Boy Scouts of America and the Campfire Girls. Died in Detroit, Michigan.

Chief Dan George

Coast Salish (20th century)

Hereditary chief. Perhaps best known for his role in the movie *Little Big Man*. Tried to use his writings and media roles to give an accurate depiction of American Indian beliefs and values.

Chief Joseph

Nez Perce (1840–1904)

Best known for his extraordinary attempt to lead his tribe through the western Rockies to Canada to escape the approaching U.S. Army. They were desperate to avoid being forced onto reservations. After three months, they were caught, and Joseph lived out his life on a reservation. He visited Washington, D.C., the year before he died.

Chief Luther Standing Bear
Oglala Sioux (1868–1939)
Wished for his people to live a nomadic lifestyle, but tried to accommodate to white ways by attending Carlisle Indian School and encouraging his people to take up farming. Turned away from white culture after witnessing the slaughter of unarmed men, women, and children at Wounded Knee in 1890. Published a book, *My Indian Boyhood,* in 1933.

Chief Plenty Coups (Aleek-chea-ahoosh)
Crow (1849–1932)
A warrior, but never fought against the white man. Became a chief at only twenty-five years of age. He was one of the first of his people to take up farming and ranching. Was said to have eleven wives, but no children. Willed his land to the American people as a memorial park to the Crow Nation. It is now a museum.

Chief Seattle
Suqwamish and Duwamish (1786–1866)
Seattle was a Christian and an ally of the white man. He agreed to settle the Washington tribes on reservations in 1855. He gave a speech to the governor of Washington Territory in 1853.

Cochise ("Like Ironweed")
Chiricahua Apache Chief
(date of birth unknown–1874)
Originally acquiesced to the white advance across the Southwest. Turned against the Americans when his people were falsely accused of kidnapping a young boy. Subsequently fought the whites for many years in the Southwest. He and his warriors were legendary for their surprise attacks, uncompromising ruthlessness in pursuit of their own goals, and knowledge of their own land. He died a natural death.

Crow Belly
Gros Ventre Chief (mid-19th century)

Crowfoot
Blackfeet Chief (late 19th century)
Crowfoot was a hunter and warrior who ceded the

land of his people to the Canadian government without realizing what he was doing.

Four Guns
Oglala Sioux (late 19th century)
A judge.

George Copway (Kahgegagahbowh)
Ojibwe (ca. 1818–ca. 1863)
One of the first Indian writers to be widely read by whites. Born in Ontario to a hereditary chief, and became a missionary. Translated religious texts into Ojibwe.

George Henry
Ojibwe Methodist Preacher.

Gertrude S. Bonnin (Zitkala-Sa)
Yankton Sioux (1875–1938)
Teacher, musician and writer. Educated by Quakers, and taught at Carlisle Indian School in Pennsylvania. Wrote articles for Harper's and Atlantic. Activist in political affairs. Founded Council of American Indians.

Joseph Brant (Thayendanegea)
Mohawk (ca. 1742–1807)
Dedicated his life to the fight for the right of the Five

Nations to be free. He was an intellectual, a military strategist, and a translator of religious documents. He was the most famous war chief of the Five Nations in their fight to ward off the advancing Europeans. Later, he decided to fight on the side of the British in the Revolutionary War after a fact-finding mission to England. He was no stranger to Washington, D.C., and it was there that he was known for his eloquence and good sense. He died in battle.

Kanekuk
Kickapoo prophet (ca. 1785–1852)
Tribal chief, religious pacifist. Encouraged farming among his people and received assistance from the federal government as a result. His people were finally forced off their land by encroaching white settlers. Died of smallpox.

King Hendrick (Tiyanoga)
Mohawk (ca. 1680–1755)
Once met Queen Anne in England, and thereafter was dubbed "King Hendrick." Criticized British army strategy against the French in North America. Died in battle against the French.

King Wahunsonacook
Powhatan
Led a confederacy of thirty-two bands. Had twenty

sons and eleven daughters, one of whom was Pocahontas. To gain his support for their settlement at Jamestown, the English placed a gold crown on his head and proclaimed him "King Powhatan."

Long Mandan
Sioux
Opposed the white attempts to take the Black Hills of South Dakota, which the Sioux considered the sacred center of the world.

Many Horses
Oglala Sioux (date of birth unknown–1867)
War chief and wealthy breeder of horses, which he acquired in raids. Killed in battle.

Maquinna
Nootka Chief (early 19th century)
Attacked a trading ship in 1803, and killed the entire crew except for two people. One of the captives wrote an account which was widely read by whites.

Peter Jones
(Kahkewaquonaby or Sacred Waving Feathers)
Ojibwe (1802–1856)
Author of *A History of the Ojhibwe Indian*, still a highly

regarded text. An Episcopal minister and a missionary to Eastern Ontario. Traveled extensively, to New York, London, and many other cities.

Red Cloud
Oglala Sioux (ca. 1822–1909)
Red Cloud initially believed that making peace with the white government was the only way to promote an orderly passage of whites through Indian land. But unkept treaty promises prompted him to take up arms and fight the whites in 1866. After humiliating General Sherman with his military forays, he again promoted a just peace and led a group called Red Cloud's Peace Crusade to Washington, D.C., in 1870. The government's failure to live up to its promises a second time left him embittered. He remained a spokesman for his people until his death.

Red Dog
Oglala Sioux (19th century)
Red Dog was adamantly opposed to the white miners and settlers who poured into the Black Hills of South Dakota in search of gold. He was an eloquent spokesman for Indian rights who consistently confronted the white government for its betrayal of its treaty obligations.

Red Jacket (Sa-Go-Ye-Wat-Ha)
Seneca (1756–1830)

Red Jacket was a warrior and an orator. He spent several weeks in Washington, D.C., where he met with President George Washington and addressed the U.S. Senate. He was open about his contempt for the white man's religion.

Satank
Kiowa (ca. 1810–1871)

Satank negotiated a peace treaty between the Kiowas and the Cheyennes. However, he was not a peacemaker with the white man. Though he knew that his people could not drive the whites away, he led raids against the settlers in an attempt to stop their fencing of the land and killing of game. He was eventually captured. Even then, he attacked a guard on his way to prison and was shot to death. His body was thrown in a ditch.

Satanta
Kiowa Chief (ca. 1830–1878)

Sometimes called the "Orator of the Plains." He fought against the westward expansion of the railroads because he knew they would disrupt the buffalo herds that were the basis of Kiowa survival. He was taken prisoner by General Sherman, who tricked him with false claims of a peaceful council meeting. He committed suicide while imprisoned in Texas.

Sharitarish
Pawnee (ca. 1790–1822)
Met Zebulon Pike in Nebraska. Delivered a speech to President Monroe about self-determination. Died of cholera.

Simon Pokagon
Potawatomi Chief (1830–1899)
Lecturer and writer. Educated at Notre Dame. Was a professional organist and spoke five languages fluently. Met with both President Lincoln and President Grant.

Sitting Bull (Tatanka Yotanka)
Teton Sioux (late 19th century)
A medicine man and tribal chief. He consistently explained to the whites that he did not wish to fight them, but only to hunt on his own land. Eventually the Teton Sioux prevailed upon him to become their war chief when the whites insisted on wantonly killing the buffalo and despoiling grazing lands. He is best known for his defeat of Custer at the Battle of Little Big Horn, and for his endurance in the Sun Dance. He is considered to be the last Sioux to surrender to the U.S.

government. He was murdered by tribal police who were sent to arrest him.

Tecumseh
Shawnee (1768–1813)
Tecumseh spent his life trying to convince the Six Nations to ally themselves with the Indians in the Ohio and Mississippi Valleys to stop the white man. He was a highly respected warrior and statesman, and was a commissioned brigadier general in the British armed forces in Canada. He was killed in battle in Ontario.

Teedyuscung
Delaware (ca. 1705–1763)
Tribal chief. Fought to keep his people's land. Converted to Christianity, but later went back to his traditional way of life. Sided with the British against the French. Was a heavy drinker, but still respected. Burned to death in his home as a result of a fire set by a personal enemy.

Ten Bears
Yamparika Comanche (1792–1872)
More a poet than a warrior, he was considered a great peacemaker. He spent his life seeking concessions from Washington and keeping the Comanches from going to

war. He was largely unsuccessful, but was admired by everyone for his heroic efforts. He died a bitter man.

Tomochichi
Creek Chief (ca. 1650–1739)
Friendly to colonists. Traveled to England, where he gave numerous speeches. Initiated trade between England and his people.

White Shield
Arikara (Southern Cheyenne) Chief
(ca. 1833–1883)
Peacemaker. Met with President Grant. Opposed white ranchers being allowed to graze their cattle on his people's lands.

Wovoka
Paiute (late 19th century)
Known as "The Paiute Messiah." Fell ill with a fever during a solar eclipse in 1889 and thereafter had visions. Preached that the Great Spirit would restore Indian people to their former glory if they all participated in the Ghost Dance. The Ghost Dance became a great religious ceremony among the plains Indians in the 1890s.

ADDITIONAL NOTES

Constitution of the Five Nations
The Five Nations of the Cayuga, Mohawk, Oneida, Onondaga, and Seneca formed the Iroquois Confederation long before Columbus set foot on America. They later became known as the Six Nations when the Tuscarora joined the Confederation. Their constitution was used by Benjamin Franklin as a model for the Articles of Confederation.

Treaty negotiations with the Six Nations were in the early to mid-18th century.

The Sioux tribes were sometimes called the Dakota. They originally inhabited the Upper Midwest. They are sometimes divided into three dialect groups, each group consisting of several tribes:

(1) The Dakota are the Santee or Eastern group, composed of the Mdewakanton, Sisseton, Wahpeton, and Wahpehnta tribes.

(2) The Nakota is the Middle group, composed of the Yankton and Yanktonai tribes.

(3) The Lakota is the Teton or Western group, composed of the Oglala, Brule, Hunkpapa, Miniconjon, Sans Arcs, Sihasapa (or Blackfoot), and Two Kettle tribes.

The quote about the Indians turning down the offer to send their young men to school took place in 1744, when commissioners from Maryland and Virginia offered to send Indian boys to William and Mary College.

ABOUT THE EDITOR

Kent Nerburn holds a Ph.D. in Religion and Art. He is an internationally recognized artist with sculptures in such settings as Westminster Benedictine Abbey in Mission, British Columbia, and the Peace Museum in Hiroshima, Japan. For several years he worked with the Ojibwe of northern Minnesota helping collect the memories of their tribal elders.

He is the author of *Neither Wolf nor Dog: On Forgotten Roads with an Indian Elder, A Haunting Reverence, Small Graces, Simple Truths, Letters to My Son,* and *Make Me an Instrument of Your Peace.*

He lives with his wife, Louise Mengelkoch, and their son, Nicholas, in northern Minnesota.

New World Library is dedicated to publishing books
and cassettes that inspire and challenge us to improve
the quality of our lives and the world.

New World Library
14 Pamaron Way
Novato, CA 94949

Phone: (415) 884-2100
Fax: (415) 884-2199
Or call toll-free (800) 972-6657
Catalog Requests: Ext. 50
Ordering: Ext. 52

E-mail: escort@nwlib.com
http://www.nwlib.com